Studies in Empirical Economics

Aman Ullah (Ed.)
Semiparametric and Nonparametric Econometrics
1989. VII, 172 pp. Hard cover DM 120,–
ISBN 3-7908-0418-5

Walter Krämer (Ed.)
Econometrics of Structural Change
1989. X, 128 pp. Hard cover DM 85,–
ISBN 3-7908-0432-0

Wolfgang Franz (Ed.)
Hysteresis Effects in Economic Models
1990. VIII, 121 pp. Hard cover DM 90,–
ISBN 3-7908-0482-7

John Piggott and John Whalley (Eds.)
Applied General Equilibrium
1991. VI, 153 pp. Hard cover DM 98,–
ISBN 3-7908-0530-0

Baldev Raj and Badi H. Baltagi (Eds.)
Panel Data Analysis
1992. VIII, 220 pp. Hard cover DM 128,–
ISBN 3-7908-0593-9

Josef Christl
The Unemployment / Vacancy Curve
1992. XVI, 152 pp. Hard cover DM 98,–
ISBN 3-7908-0625-0

Jürgen Kaehler and Peter Kugler (Eds.)
Econometric Analysis of Financial Markets
1994. VII, 230 pp. Hard cover DM 98,–
ISBN 3-7908-0740-0

Klaus F. Zimmermann (Ed.)
Output and Employment Fluctuations
1994. VI, 259 pp. Hard cover DM 128,–
ISBN 3-7908-0754-0

Jean-Marie Dufour and Baldev Raj (Eds.)
New Developments in Time Series Econometrics
1994. V, 250 pp. Hard cover DM 148,–
ISBN 3-7908-0766-4

John D. Hey (Ed.)

Experimental Economics

With 13 Figures

Springer-Verlag Berlin Heidelberg GmbH

Editor
Professor John D. Hey
Department of Economics
University of York
Heslington, York Y01 5DD
United Kingdom

First published in "Empirical Economics"
Vol. 19, No. 2, 1994

ISBN 978-3-642-51181-3 ISBN 978-3-642-51179-0 (eBook)
DOI 10.1007/978-3-642-51179-0

CIP-Titelaufnahme der Deutschen Bibliothek

Experimental economics / John D. Hey (ed.). – Heidelberg:
Physica-Verl., 1994
(Studies in empirical economics)

NE: Hey, John D. [Hrsg.]

Originally published by Physica-Verlag Heidelberg in 1994.

88/2202-543210 – Printed on acid-free paper

Preface

When I was invited by Andreas Wörgötter to edit a volume in the "Studies in Empirical Economics" series devoted to Experimental Economics, I was both flattered and excited: flattered that I was to be entrusted with such a task for a series with high standards and proud history of such volumes; excited by the prospect of drawing together new material in this fascinating, challenging and important area of economics. With some trepidation, I drew up a list of the most active experimental economists throughout the world and invited the top ten or so to contribute. I was delighted by the response: no doubt drawn by the attraction of the series, a gratifyingly large proportion accepted.

Most, but not all (though I will not name the guilty parties!) delivered on time and with the appropriate quality. All were very responsive to my editorial suggestions, and the following is the result. It is an exciting glimpse of what is going on in this key area of economics. I, and the authors, hope that it will encourage the continuing growth of interest in experimental economics.

My thanks to Andreas Wörgötter for his help and encouragement throughout – and for the initial invitation.

John D. Hey
University of York

Contents

Introduction and Overview

JOHN D. HEY

Department of Economics, University of York, Heslington, York Y01 5DD, United Kingdom

The time has probably come for Experimental Economics to stop saying that it is a young branch of economics, and for it to claim, quite correctly, that it is a maturing subject. This is not to say that it is growing old, or intellectually dying, but rather that it is entering a new phase where the early doubts (both within the experimental community and without) have been resolved, where the enormous potential of the experimental approach is being increasingly appreciated, and where this potential is being explored with increasing vigour and confidence. It is an exciting time to be an experimental economist.

The beginning of the coming-of-age of Experimental Economics is witnessed in part by the publication of a number of textbooks and collections of papers. There is my own textbook (Hey 1991) and very good texts by Davis and Holt (1993) and by Friedman and Sunder (1994). There are collections of papers by Smith (1990 and 1991) and by Hey and Loomes (1993). And soon, we hope, there will be the definitive *Handbook of Experimental Economics* (Kagel and Roth, forthcoming) which will be a mine of useful information about what has been done in the field in the past. Of course, papers on and using experimental methods appear in all the top-rank journals (and elsewhere) and, from time to time, there are special issues in the *Journal of Economic Behavior and Organization* specifically devoted to Experimental Economics

Now there is *this* volume in the "Studies in Empirical Economics" series devoted to Experimental Economics. When inviting me to act as Editor for this volume, Andreas Wörgötter gave me essentially an editorially free hand. I chose to use this wonderful opportunity to show what is going on at the frontiers in this subject, and to show what the top experimental economists are currently thinking and doing. This is a *looking forward* volume, not a looking back one. The material is innovative, in many different ways. I hope it conveys some glimpse of the vision of what is achievable with experimental methods.

While the unifying feature of the papers in this volume is that they are all innovative, they are innovative in different ways: Bohm tackles an old and familiar issue using a new experimental technology; Burrows and Loomes take the experimental analysis of a theoretically new area one stage further, thereby carefully distinguishing between competing hypotheses; Harrison re-interprets old evidence from a new perspective and comes up with fresh conclusions which he then subjects to test; Lim, Prescott and Sunder venture into a new area for experimentalists – that of overlapping generations models – and shows how experiments can shed light where theory cannot; Roth makes an impassioned plea for a new methodological approach, or rather a new approach to the reporting of experiments; Sbriglia and Hey take experimental economics into uncharted waters – by running ill-defined experiments. These are, perhaps, the visions of the future.

Whilst the various papers can speak better for themselves than I can, it may prove useful to those readers whose time is scarce to give a brief overview of the various contributions here. I do so in no particular intellectual order, but in the order in which the papers appear, which is alphabetical by lead author.

The Bohm paper revisits old and familiar ground: that of *preference reversals.* This is a phenomenon which is now established both in economics and psychology as an 'established truth' and is as follows. Subjects are confronted with two choices (usually risky, but this is not necessary) A and B. They are first asked to state whether they prefer A to B or *vice versa.* They are then asked to state selling prices on both A and B: P_A and P_B respectively. Often it is observed that $A > B$ whilst $P_A < P_B$; this contradicts many standard theories of choice. Much work, of both an experimental and theoretical nature, has been done, respectively testing for the robustness of this phenomenon and exploring the implications for the theory of choice. Bohm's starting point is that much of the experimental work, in his opinion, is of rather dubious validity – mainly because of the rather trivial nature of A and B used in many experiments. To test this he implements a new type of experiment in which A and B are of serious concern *to the subjects participating in the experiment.* He finds that the preference reversal phenomenon disappears. We await the reaction of the experimental community!

The Burrows and Loomes paper, although less overtly controversial, is also addressed to a controversial issue: the relative superiority of 'neo-classical' solutions to bargaining problems vis-a-vis more sociological or psychological solutions incorporating notions of fairness. Moreover, they take the argument a stage further – by designing their experiment in such a way that they can distinguish between different motivations for fairness. Their results shed interesting light on the question of whether unequal incomes arrived at by luck are considered less fair by subjects than unequal incomes arrived at through work or expertise. This paper demonstrates with great clarity how experiments can be carefully designed to test between closely competitive hypotheses; something that may well not be possible, particularly in the bargaining context, with conventional data.

Harrison's paper is methodologically very close to Bohm's – which is perhaps not surprising since Bohm and Harrison often work together. Like Bohm, Harrison picks an area where, largely by virtue of past experimental work, economists and psychologists have converged on an 'established truth' – but one which is of dubious validity to Harrison, again by virtue of design problems with the experiments that were instrumental in 'establishing' it. In this case, the 'established truth' is the inapplicability – as a descriptive device – of Expected Utility (EU) Theory. For over three decades now, staring with the celebrated

Allais paradox, EU theory has been under assault – both from experimentalists and theoreticians. A whole industry has evolved, producing alternatives to, and generalisations of, EU theory. Harrison is dubious, for a variety of reasons, but most importantly because of what he terms the 'flat maximum critique'. This critique is applied to those experiments where the design is such that subjects can stray a long way from the payment maximising decision with relatively trivial reductions to their actual payments. Accordingly, one should have little confidence in their actual decisions.

Lim, Prescott and Sunder's paper takes us back into less controversial territory, but one that is no less innovative. Their experiments relate to the rapidly expanding theoretical literature on Overlapping Generations (OLG) models, the over-riding feature of which is their multiple equilibria (or indeterminacy of equilibrium). Since theory sheds little light on to which of many equilibria might be attained, they turn to experiments to see if they shed any light. Indeed they do. And, in the meantime, Lim, Prescott and Sunder give useful advice on how to replicate OLG models in the laboratory.

Roth's paper stands out from the others as it involves no fresh experimental results. Yet it makes a profound methodological point: one should be equally careful in reporting experimental results as econometricians *should be* in reporting econometric results. The title of his paper echoes the title of one of a number of papers exploring the issue from the econometricians' point of view. The moral is clear: one should be as honest in reporting 'unsuccessful' experiments as one is in reporting 'successful' experiments. But will journal editors allow the space?

Sbriglia and Hey's paper takes experiments into relatively uncharted waters: those of 'ill-defined' experiments. Such experiments may be ill-defined in one of a number of ways. In the experiments reported in this paper, it is the nature of the 'optimal strategy' for subjects to follow that which is ill-defined. Despite repeated attempts by economic theorists, an optimal strategy to the problem set to the subjects in the experiment described in this paper has yet to be found. This really is the essence of the experiment; most crucially it provides an antidote to recent theory in Industrial Organisation addressed to the R & D problem. Sbriglia and Hey's starting point is the idea that the crucial problem faced by those engaging in R & D activity is that their problem *cannot* be formulated in the well-defined manner beloved by neoclassical economic theorists: there are not well-defined "rules of the game". Hence, even if the decision-maker has a well-defined objective function, the concept of an 'optimal strategy' to tackle the problem is not well-defined.

More generally, an ill-defined experiment is one in which either the "rules of the game" are incompletely specified (and hence have to be discovered by the subjects) or the 'optimal strategy' (if one does indeed 'exist') is so complex that its solution is outwith the capabilities of the subjects. In such experiments, the experimenter, *a fortiori*, cannot be testing whether behaviour accords with some optimising theory, but is rather testing some other type of theory, or, more primitively, trying to discover a 'theory' which might describe the behaviour of the subjects. In this sense, such experiments are 'theory-discovering' rather than 'theory-testing'. I see considerable potential for such experiments.

At the same time, the future will continue to witness the growth of theory-testing experiments. As the experiments reported in this volume demonstrate clearly, the experimental approach facilitates great precision in distinguishing between theories. Thus, both this kind of experiment, and the more speculative ill-defined, possibly theory-suggesting, experiments, will contribute to the strengthening of the theoretical foundations of economics. I hope that this volume will play a modest role in this process.

References

Davis DD, Holt CA (1993) Experimental economics. Princeton UP
Friedman JW, Sunder S (1994) Experimental economics. Cambridge UP
Hey JD (1991) Experimental economics. Blackwells
Hey JD Loomes GC (1993) Recent developments in experimental economics (2 vols) Edward Elgar
Kagel JH, Roth AE (forthcoming) Handbook of experimental economics. Princeton UP
Smith VL (1990) Experimental economics. Edward Elgar
Smith VL (1991) Papers in experimental economics. Cambridge UP

Behaviour under Uncertainty without Preference Reversal: A Field Experiment

PETER BOHM[1]

Department of Economics, University of Stockholm, 10691 Stockholm, Sweden

Abstract: The robust laboratory evidence of preference reversal for lotteries has been interpreted as a threat to the general validity of standard theories of decision-making under uncertainty. This evidence is obtained from laboratory, that is, not real-world, lotteries with subjects who have not sought to make decisions among such lotteries. Here, the prevalence of preference reversal is studied in a field experiment with used cars, that is, a case of real-world non-trivial, non-lottery – but still payoff-uncertain – choice objects, and with subjects who registered as potential buyers of such cars. No sign of preference reversal was observed.

JEL-Classification System-Numbers: C93, D1, D80

Inconsistency between choice and valuation – or preference reversal – was first observed by psychologists in laboratory experiments with lotteries at the beginning of the 70s. Their reports met with scepticism from economists, partly perhaps because preference reversal would mean a blow to a vital part of standard economic theory. However, once preference reversal was replicated by economists in lottery experiments, which were carefully checked against a set of potential mistakes in experimental design (see Grether and Plott, 1979), the phenomenon has been accepted by a large number of economists. For some time now a major preoccupation in this field has been to find an explanation of the phenomenon. Is it the transitivity, independence, asymmetry or some other axiom that is violated by preference reversal (see Loomes and Sugden, 1983, Holt, 1986, Karni and Safra, 1986, Machina, 1987, Segal, 1988, Cox and Epstein, 1989, and Loomes, Starmer and Sugden, 1989)? How much of standard decision theory can be saved? Examinations of these questions have found their way into leading economics journals, thus "confirming" the relevance and seriousness of the problem. No wonder, perhaps, since Grether and Plott argued in their seminal article that the inconsistency implied by preference reversal "is deeper than the mere lack of transitivity... It suggests that no optimization principles of any

---

[1] I am grateful to the Trygg-Hansa Foundation and the Bank of Sweden Tercentenary Foundation for financial support and to members of the Department of Economics, University of Stockholm, in particular Staffan Stockeld, Hans Lind and Lars Vahtrik, for assistance in carrying out the experiment presented here. I have benefited from helpful comments by Mats Bohman, Stefan Fölster, Glenn Harrison, James Harrison, and Hans Lind on a working paper, "Preference Reversal: What Does the Laboratory Evidence Tell Us?", 1990, of which the present paper is a shorter version.

sort lie behind even the simplest of human choices and that the uniformities in human choice behaviour may result from principles which are of a completely different sort from those generally accepted" (Grether and Plott, 1979, p. 623).

Preference reversal has been identified in a number of laboratory tests and a common verdict now is that the evidence is "robust". The psychologists Lichtenstein and Slovic, who were the first to discover preference reversal, have more recently advised economists to "accept the reality of preference reversals and related information-processing pheomena and ... explore their implications for important social and economic behaviors" (Slovic and Lichtenstein, 1983, p. 602). Nevertheless, the nature of the laboratory evidence is such that there is still considerable uncertainty as to what real-world phenomena the robust evidence is actually valid for, and exactly what we are invited to accept as fact. More specifically, do we know for a fact that preference reversal occurs in situations of choice with uncertain payoffs other than those situations – essentially laboratory lotteries – for which it has been found to hold?

Here, we report on a field experiment where preference reversal does not arise. In this experiment, choices refer to a non-lottery (but still outcome-uncertain) message space involving non-trivial values for decision-makers.[2] In addition, and in contrast to earlier experiments, the choices observed are those made outside the laboratory, in the sense that decision-makers, in their own self-interest, *seek* these choices. It is, of course, primarily for such situations that we want the theory to be applicable. However, when it comes to creating incentives for truthful reporting of preferences as well as truthful reporting of reservation prices in such tests, we will not be able to leave completely the laboratory nor the lottery context; in fact, it remains to be shown how the combination of such data can be obtained from the field. Still, the test objects or – in the terminology of laboratory experimentalists – the message space of the experiment presented here are not lotteries but used cars, notoriously uncertain in their provision of future services to their users.

In Section I we give the background to the choice of the experimental design, the details of which are presented in Section II. The results of the test are set forth in Section III. The implications of these results are discussed in a concluding section.

I The Objective of the Experiment

Typical for most of the experiments used for testing preference reversal are choices between a P bet (a lottery with a high probability of winning a small

[2] For a definition of "message space" see Smith (1982).

amount, say, a 35/36 chance of winning \$4 and a 1/36 chance of losing \$1) and a \$ bet (a low probability of winning a relatively large amount, say, a 11/36 chance of winning \$16 and a 25/36 chance of losing \$1.50) and eliciting selling reservation prices for each of these lotteries.[3] Preference reversal, that is, subjects stating lower prices for the preferred lottery, has typically been observed in more than 30 percent of the cases and as much as some 70 percent of the cases where P bets are preferred. The most important characteristics of these lotteries can be summarized as follows:

a) Only "homemade" lotteries have been used as choice objects. They do not represent real-world lotteries, primarily because (1) the price for the the laboratory lottery ticket is zero, implying an expected loss for the lottery organization, (2) there is only one (positive) prize, and (3) prizes are trivially low. P bets of the kind used in these laboratory experiments are those for which preference reversal has been most prominent by far, but also those particularly hard to imagine as attractive lotteries in the real world. Since there is only one prize and, in this case, a probability of winning well above 1/2 and since real-world lotteries typically return as little as 50 percent of receipts as prizes, the prize can barely exceed the price of the lottery ticket.
b) The experimental lotteries do not well represent objects central to the theory of decision-making under uncertainty, such as financial assets, contingent contract for delivery of services, insurance policies and products with uncertain service prospects, for which there are no objective probabilities for different outcomes. Moreover, there are typically more than two outcomes for such choice objects.
c) As already noted, outcomes, that is, lottery prizes, have typically been insignificant. Thus, also the expected values of the laboratory lotteries have been very small. In addition, the difference between the expected values for the two lotteries, which the subject is asked to choose between and state reservation prices for, have in most cases been trivial. (In the example given above, the difference between the expected values is one cent.) In such cases, preference reversal may simply be the result of lack of saliency.
d) Subjects have been asked to participate in experiments concerning decision-making under uncertainty often without being told that they are supposed to choose among lotteries. Moreover, they are typically promised a payment for participating. Noting (1) that decision-makers who do not want to buy lottery tickets may behave in a way that systematically differs from those who do and, if so, (2) that theory of decision-making refers only to the latter of these two groups, we have no way of knowing to what extent participants belong to the latter group, and specifically, to what extent preference reversal occurs in that particular group.

---

[3] This representative example is taken from Grether and Plott, op.cit. For a fuller presentation of the history of preference reversal experiments, see e.g. Loomes, Starmer, and Sugden, 1989.

The objective of the experiment to be presented here is to try to avoid the characteristics mentioned above. First, the objective is to observe the consistency between choice and reservation prices concerning *non-trivial* objects the future performance of which can take on *many alternative* states or values and where the probabilities of the occurrence of these states are *subjective* only. Second, the objects were such that, due to expected differences in individual preferences, all subjects would hardly *want to* rank them in the same order and *few* subjects would be *indifferent* between them. Third, an attempt was made to use as subjects people who actually *seek* to make decisions concerning the choice objects used.

A test was arranged where the choice objects were used cars, that is, objects for which the future performance or service prospects are uncertain. Two cars – one capable of being a P bet and the other a $ bet – were bought by the experimenters in the open market for some $1,200 (SEK 8,000)[4], a price that was not disclosed to the participants. This type of cars, more than ten years old and run for more than 180,000 kms, does not have a precise market price; depending on the quality of such old cars the price could be anything from, say, $2,500 down to zero (or lower). The cars were to be auctioned off. Interested students were invited to participate in the auction.

II The Experimental Design

The test was arranged as follows:

1. In mid-May, students at the University of Stockholm were told through information sheets handed to them that those interested in buying "an inexpensive used car" should check the cars offered for sale by the Department of Economics as a part of a study of buying behaviour at this department. To be eligible, participants had to have a driver's license and be able to attend a couple of meetings, one for explaining the auction procedure that was to be used, one for test driving the cars and one for the real auction (see Appendix A for the leaflet text.) About 1500 copies were distributed. Thirty-three responded by returning signed leaflet coupons. Twenty-six persons completed the test, most of them students of Business Administration (11) and Economics (9); only 6 (23 percent) came from other disciplines (Computer Science 2, Mathematics, Chemistry, Geography and Statistics, 1 each).
2. The information meeting, held a couple of days later, took 30 minutes. The participants were told that two cars (so far unspecified) were available, one of

[4] All amounts are in 1990 prices.

which might actually be *given* away in a lottery! Thus, possibly only one would be auctioned off. All this would take place five days later. For the lottery, we needed to know which car they preferred or whether they were indifferent between the two cars.

a) A first lottery would select a "winner" (the registration number of a participant). The winner would have a 2/3 chance of winning the preferred car and a 1/3 chance of winning the other car. (Or 1/2 chance for each car, if the winner had indicated indifference.)
b) Once the prize car had been identified (through the second lottery just indicated), a third lottery was used to determine whether the winner would be allowed to keep the car (chance 1/2) or receive the price he had offered for this car (chance 1/2). Therefore, when asked to state their *buying* prices for each car, subjects were told that their bid would be used also as their *selling* price, in case they turned out to be the winner (eventually a 1/26 chance) and the prize car had to be resold (eventually a 1/52 chance). In this latter case, the car would be auctioned off, the highest bidder paying the second highest bid and the winner receiving a prize equal to his bid for this car. (The experimenter would receive the difference between the price paid by the highest bidder and the winner's bid.)

3. Thus, the subjects were told that, at the final meeting, they would be asked to state in writing (a) their preferences and (b) their bids (for the forms used, see appendix B). Moreover, they were explicitly asked to check both statements before turning them over to the experimenter.
4. Subjects were told that auctions would be of the second-price type and also what that meant in terms of incentives to state their willingness to pay as compared to the case of first-price auctions (see e.g. Vickrey, 1961).
5. At the information meeting,

a) all important information was repeated; a hypothetical trial run was arranged, observing all essential formalities (with bicycles as choice objects for illustration),
b) information was provided about special cases such as

- the possible existence of more than one highest bidder,
- the lottery winner also being the highest bidder on a prize car (if it was to be auctioned off),
- the winner of a car "for keeps" also being the highest bidder on the second car (the person who got the first car would be automatically excluded from the second round), etc.

c) a memorandum was distributed at the end of the meeting, summarizing the main points of the oral information given and including "reminders" such as (i) that they should take into account that the cars might be of interest to them either for their personal use or as a piece of property for (immediate) sale on the open market and (ii) the double role of the bids as a buying price and a potential selling price (see Appendix C),

d) people were told *now* that, if they returned for the final meeting and completed their statements, they would receive SEK 50 (about $8) for participating, and
e) participants signed up for test drives some time during the next 48 hours.

6. Finally, the car models were identified to the participants. Futhermore, copies of the test results from *two* inspection-stations (one test very detailed) of each car were given to the participants. As already mentioned, it was never disclosed what the cars cost us to buy or that we had chosen cars which had the *same price* (SEK 8,000).[5]

The test – or, as it would now appear to the informed participants, the lottery-preceded auction – was carried out as indicated and as specified in Appendix C.[6]

Some important points of the test design should now bc cxplaincd:

Why a lottery and why give away a car? We had to make it worthwhile for the subjects to reveal truthfully their preferences for the two cars. A lottery – with a significantly higher probability of winning the preferred car (if one car is preferred) than the one not preferred – was arranged for this reason.[7]

It should be noted here that the incentive mechanisms provided by this lottery and the other two (see below) imply that subjects, when choosing between cars, are asked to choose between two compound lotteries. Most previous laboratory tests also involved choosing between compound lotteries. But the important difference is that the objects in message space – or the explicit choice objects – no longer are lotteries but used cars.

Why give any chance of winning the car not preferred and why introduce the possibility of winning the money value of the bid on this car? The reason is that this adds to the incentive to make a well-considered bid also on the least preferred car. (Should preference reversal appear, it would be important to know if bids on the two cars were close or wide apart.) Now, bid levels are important for the subject if he turns out to win – not a car – but the money value of his bid for

[5] The task of a preference-reversal analyst is of course to avoid a set of alternatives (a) for which preference reversal would not really surprise anyone (that is, where the decision-maker finds the two objects so similar that he does not care whether he states preference for one object or the other or whether he makes bids that are almost but not exactly equal; cf. Pommerehne et al, 1982, and Reilly, 1982) or (b) for which absence of preference reversal is self-evident (as with a fairly new Rolls Royce and an old VW Beetle). Our choice of cars was made in an attempt to create a test situation that avoids these two extremes.

[6] Details of the manuscript of the experimenter's oral presentation are available on request.

[7] To reiterate: The prospect of winning a car or its money value – as well as the existence of a remuneration for participation – was not made known to potential participants before they registered. Hence, it is still possible to regard all participants as real consumers, that is, people interested in buying an inexpensive used car, and not as gamblers or income earners.

this car. Of course, incentives to make careful bids exist already for both cars, *provided* the respondent thinks he stands some chance of coming out on top in an auction of any one of them. This proviso is important, in particular perhaps concerning the car of his second choice, that is, the car he does not think so highly of. If, on the other hand, he feels more or less certain that his true highest bid is far below the top bids made by others – not unlikely perhaps since he does not fancy this car – he may not feel inclined to devote time and energy to investigating what his willingness to pay (WTP) for this car is. Introducing the fact that he may win the money value of his bid on the car he does not prefer, he is likely to consider more carefully his bid on this car, for example, by taking the trouble of obtaining outside information about what he could get for the car on the open market.

Could using bids also as selling prices in the way now described stop bids from being set equal to WTP, the dominating bidding strategy of the second-price auction? There is a 1/78 chance (2/3 × 1/2 × 1/26) that the bidder will win the first lottery *and* get the money value of his bid on the car he prefers or, more important for preference reversal, a 1/156 chance that he will get the money value of his bid on the least preferred car. These small chances would hardly make him raise his bid on any of the two cars above this WTP, since this would mean that he runs a risk of winning an auction at a price exceeding his WTP.

Why not ask for selling prices especially since this is what we really want, recalling that preference reversal arises and expected-utility theory is contradicted if the less-preferred car has the higher *selling* price? Any design we could think of, creating a real demand for a selling price to be used in an auction of the car prize, would provide incentives for making distorted statements. More specifically, the reason for not asking for (separate) selling prices is the potential presence of speculative considerations, creating a risk for false observations of preference reversal. For example: Car A is preferred by a person who, in addition, believes that others have a relatively much higher WTP for car B and state higher *buying* prices for car B than he does. Hence, maximizing his expected payoff, this kind of speculation can make him report a higher *selling* price for B than for A, his preferred choice.

Is it acceptable to substitute the rank order of buying prices for the rank order of selling prices? The incentive for truthfully reporting buying prices is the assumption that nobody likes to end up paying more than his WTP and that nobody – in a second-price auction – would like to make bids understating his WTP. One major reason why the buying price under the given conditions could still deviate from the selling price is related to the role of income effects. Especially, since the significance of the choice objects is one of the aspects emphasized and strived for in this study, it would not be surprising, of course, if income effects turned out to be significant.

First, however, it should be noted that the only income effects that would be troublesome here are those which would cause an unobserved *shift* from preference reversal to lack of such reversal (or vice versa). But income effects are unlikely to change the *rank order* of reservation prices, be it selling or buying prices, for such close substitutes as used cars of about the same age and "market price".

Second, the income effects may after all be rather limited, given that the market price for the cars, SEK 8,000, (although not mentioned to the participants) is likely to be the upper bound to the bids and that the minimum annual budget of a student contemplating the use of a car is likely to be on the order of SEK 50,000. Hence, winning one of these two cars would mean a net addition to "income" of at most some 15 percent. Furthermore, the relevant income concept is certainly elusive here, since it could be argued that expenditure during the years of university training should be related to income during a number of years, possibly even expected life-time income. In the perspective now proposed, it hardly seems controversial to make the assumption that the selling price for a car, if you had won it and thus had your "income" increased with this prize, equals approximately the buying price at the initially given income.

Summing up, it seems unlikely that disregarding (small) income effects would distort the observed rate of preference reversal. It might be added that in some of the previous preference reversal experiments both buying prices (or "equivalents") and selling prices were elicited (for example, Slovic and Lichtenstein, 1968, Lichtenstein and Slovic, 1971, and Grether and Plott, 1979). A considerable rate of preference reversal was observed also for buying prices (sometimes higher and sometimes lower than for selling prices), indicating that the use of buying prices did not stop preference reversal from arising in lottery experiments.[8]

III Results

The choices and bids are shown in Table 1, with the bid for the preferred car underlined. As it turned out, the winner in the lottery got the car he did not

[8] All risks that preference reversals go unnoticed have not been possible to avoid with the experimental design used here. Assuming that an individual is a preference reverser, so that he actually prefers car A to car B and would like to state a price for B, p(B), higher than that for A, p(A), it may happen that he now wants to state a preference for car B. The reason is as follows: By choosing to state B he increases the chances of winning the money value of B (= his bid on B) which is higher than his bid on A. More specifically, in the particular case of preference reversal where he values the difference p(B) vs p(A) more than car A vs car B, he would indeed want to state a preference for B. – The problem with this line of reasoning, however, is that the rationality that is assumed for his choice of response just indicated was not assumed to hold for his "actual" preferences for the cars and his "actual" reservation prices. Once we wish to deviate from one implication of standard theory (assuming preference reversal behavior), it is hard to know when, if ever, other implications of that theory can be relied upon to hold.

Table 1. Bids (in SEK) and preferences (indicated by figures underlined)

Participant no.	Opel	Volvo	Participant no.	Opel	Volvo
1^{e}	1,100	1,100 <	14^{b}	1,000	<u>1,500</u>
2^{e}	500	<u>1,000</u>	15^{b}	2,000	<u>2,600</u>
3^{e}	4,300	<u>4,300</u> <	16^{e}	6,100	<u>6,100</u> <
4^{b}	500	<u>3,800</u>	17°	1,200	<u>3,100</u>
5°	1,100	<u>1,200</u>	18^{b}	500	<u>700</u>
6^{b}	2,600	<u>3,300</u>	19^{e}	500	<u>600</u>
7°	3,400	<u>6,900</u>	20^{b}	1,000	<u>1,600</u>
8^{b}	<u>600</u>	500	21^{b}	1,800	<u>2,200</u>
9°	1,000	<u>3,000</u>	22^{e}	2,000	<u>2,000</u> <
10^{e}	900	<u>1,200</u>	23^{b}	500	<u>3,800</u>
11^{e}	<u>2,500</u>	2,000	24^{b}	100	<u>300</u>
12^{b}	<u>1,400</u>	1,300	25°	<u>5,600</u>	3,600
13°	<u>3,300</u>	3,300 <	26^{e}	3,000	<u>5,400</u>

(Indices show subjects as students of Business Administration (b), Economics (e) and from other disciplines (o). Equal bids are marked by <.)

Note that participants were anonymous to one another, that they could not check what statements and bids others made, but that they could communicate as much as they wanted from their first contact on May 24 (if they already knew each other or got acquainted then) to the final meeting on May 29 (cf. respondents 4 and 23 for a possible example of the results of a "coalition".) The possibility of an enforceable coalition among all participants was negligible.

Note also that only even SEK 100 bids were accepted; participants were told that noncompliant bids would be lowered to the nearest SEK 100 (which turned out to be necessary in one case only, no. 17).

prefer (an Opel 1977) "for keeps". Hence, only one of the cars, a Volvo 1976, was auctioned off. The highest bid here was SEK 6,900 and the second bid, hence the price paid, was SEK 6,100.[9]

Only one participant (No. 1) stated indifference between the cars. He and another four participants gave bids which did not discriminate between the cars. Thus, four persons indicated strict preferences but did not differentiate their bids between the cars; we shall return to this case below. However, no case of preference reversal occurred.

Only five out of 26 participants preferred the Opel; 20 preferred the Volvo (see Table 2). This result requires some comments: To begin with, it should be noted that the Volvo had been chosen by us as a candidate for the possible role of a P

[9] The fact that some subjects gave "ridiculously" low bids – as low as SEK 100 (no. 24) – should not be regarded as a proof that the incentives discussed in the preceding section are ineffective. There are certain used cars, of course, which some potential buyers would hardly touch, let alone be found trying to sell to someone else. To such a person, SEK 100 may be his absolute max WTP for the car concerned. (Or if one would like to limit the applicability of consumer theory to "serious" customers, one might consider excluding such outliers.)

Table 2. Relations between choices and bids

	Choices	*Bids*		
		Consistent	Inconsistent	Equal
The Volvo	20	17	0	3
The Opel	5	4	0	1
Indifferent	1	(1)	0	(1)

bet (a large probability of making a small gain) in the world of non-lottery objects with uncertain service prospects. This particular choice is backed by the fact that Volvo, a product of Sweden, in this country is considered (a) to be reliable and (b) – by young people, at least – to be a rather dull car. The other car, a "luxury" version of the Opel Rekord (inside much nicer than the Volvo – with theater-red plush upholstery and a good radio) was selected as a car that could appear as a $ bet (a small probability of making a large gain, relatively speaking!). More specifically, it would provide "high-quality" transportation services – if it kept going!

Now, as it happened, the Opel gear box broke down when test driven – which everybody except the experimenters thought was funny. (In view of the fact that these old cars were to be – and was – test driven by all subjects, we were aware of this risk and had arranged with a repair shop to have repair needs taken care of right away.) In spite of the fact that the gear box was repaired and provided with a warranty, there was a risk, of course, that the reputation of the Opel was seriously hurt by this incident. If so, the Volvo would be the obvious first choice.[10] However, it must be noted that – aside from the fact that five persons actually preferred the Opel – a fairly large number of subjects gave the same or almost the same bid on the two cars: in all, 15 subjects made bids differing by less that SEK 500. (Check also Table 3, where average bids on the first choice are shown to be almost the same, and the average bid on the second choice was clearly below that of the first choice, regardless of what the first choice was.) This hardly indicates that the Volvo was regarded as the obviously and generally better car of the two.

Table 3. Average bids

Average bid by those who prefer	the Volvo	the Opel	Neither	Total
For the Volvo:	2,730	2,140	(1,100)	2,554
For the Opel:	1,750	2,680	(1,100)	1,904

[10] It should be noted here that one of the test-stations used reported some 50 deficiences on each of the cars (using new cars as their standard of comparison). These reports along with the age and appearence of the cars clearly told the participants that both cars were capable of breaking down.

It should also be noted here that, given the interpretation of the Volvo as a P bet and the Opel as a $ bet, preference reversal has previously been observed primarily for those who rank P bets before $ bets. A typical example: in their main experiment with incentives, Grether and Plott observed preference reversal in 70 percent of the choices ranking the P bet first and in only some 15 percent of the choices ranking the $ bet first. Therefore, to test whether preference reversal at all arises in the context of used cars, we would welcome a large number of observations where P bets are preferred. As it turned out in the test presented here, most choices involved ranking that alternative first which is, at least potentially, a P bet.

Four out of 26 subjects constituted what we may call cases of "weak" preference reversal in that they preferred car A to car B while stating bids, $p(A) = p(B)$. Could this be regarded as something along the road to "strong" preference reversal? Not necessarily. First, prices or bids are relatively difficult to specify even when preferences are clear and, hence, easy to state. And bids (how much?) take more time than choice (yes/no) to specify. Hence, in principle, identical bids are compatible with strict preferences. Second, budget constraints may bind the bids to one and the same for both cars, although one of the cars is strictly preferred and would command a higher bid in the absence of a binding budget constraint. Thus, it does not seem possible to make anything significant out of this part of the results.

IV Concluding Comments

How do the results obtained here square with the results obtained earlier indicating preference reversal?

One possible explanation (pointed out by Harrison (1988) and to some extent already by Pommerehne et al. (1982)) for the preference reversals observed and reported on in the literature is related to the fact that in most of the laboratory tests, the costs of behavior inconsistent with theory have been trivial and so have the incentives to identify and report correctly preferences as well as bids (reservation prices). In contrast, given that the objects were more valuable in the test presented, participants are likely to have been more careful when judging the objects.

Another possible explanation springs from the hypothesis that (laboratory) lotteries constitute a quite special message space and fail to work well as stylized situations of choices between uncertain alternatives in general. The possibility of gambling being something special is reminiscent of the time when it was believed to be "paradoxical" that one and the same individual bought both insurance and lottery tickets, that is, seemed to be a risk lover and a risk averter at the same time. The paradox disappeared once it was realized that gambling could represent something generically different from insurance (entertainment?). Similarly, the explanation here could be that pure gambling alternatives do not well represent objects with uncertain outcomes in general. More specifically, it is now possible to argue that *preference reversal cannot be seen as a problem for behaviour under uncertainty in general as long as preference reversal has not been replicated in non-gambling situations.*

One may wonder why economists have not paid more attention to the issue of whether or not preference reversal exists outside a rather limited set of artificial environments before setting out to identify possible explanations for preference reversal under uncertainty in general (for references see the Introduction). One could, of course, take the position that preference reversal in laboratory lotteries is important *per se*. This argument could run as follows: Proponents of expected utility theory have not made reservations for certain areas of application where the theory does not hold; hence, it is important that the theory is tested for all kinds of applications, including artificial lotteries. Accepting or rejecting a position like this is essentially a matter of taste. But what is clear from the existing literature, quoted in the Introduction, is that the preference reversal issues tested in the laboratory have been taken by many, not (only) as something interesting in its own right, but as a valid representation of a wide class of real-world issues. The obvious problem with that position is that it overlooks the fact that some effort must be devoted to ascertaining explicitly what the laboratory tests actually are taken to represent.

We have seen here that the experience of preference reversal from lottery experiments need not have anything to say about the frequency, or even the existence, of such behavior outside laboratory lotteries. Therefore, for preference reversal to be acknowledged as a blow to expected-utility theory and as a general problem that decision theory has to come to grips with, real-world issues must be identified where preference reversal is actually shown to exist.

Appendix A Information Leaflet

The following text (with a different layout) was distributed to some 1500 persons, in and around the main student restaurant on the Stockholm University campus:

"In connection with *a study of buying behaviour* carried out at the Department of Economics, we ask ... Are you

INTERESTED IN BUYING AN INEXPENSIVE USED CAR FOR THE SUMMER?

If so, you have quite an *opportunity now*!

We have two cars both conscientiously tested by an "M"/corresponding to the AAA/ test station. Both cars can be test driven. Will be sold to the highest bidder. But – note – the price will be lower than that of the highest bidder!

If you are interested, complete the form attached below and return it to us/when and how/.

If the number of people interested is large, a random sample of participants will be drawn. Participants will be summoned to a 45-minute information meeting on *Wednesday, May 24 at noon.* The cars can be test driven when convenient during the period *May 24 p m to May 26 p m.*

The sealed-bid auction will take place on *Monday, May 29 at noon.* Takes some 45 minutes.

For participation it is required that you have a driver's licence and can attend the meetings mentioned! If you meet these requirements and are interested –

COMPLETE THE REGISTRATION FORM AND RETURN IT TO US AS SOON AS YOU CAN!"

REGISTRATION

I am interested in buying an inexpensive and tested used car. I can participate in the meetings mentioned! I have a driver's licence. Right now I am a student/employed at .... Department.

(Room for signature, name in block letters, address, telephone – no. and hours)

Appendix B Forms for Preference Statements and Bids

Preference statement:

"I prefer ...! (State the make of the car.)

No, I think they are equally good! (In that case check here //!)

Signature"

Bids:

/Note that the form used in the trial run did not specify the makes of the cars. The wording also reflected the fact that it was a trial run. The final version of the form ran as follows:/

"My bid on the Opel with license plates X is SEK ...

My bid on the Volvo with license plates Y is SEK ...

I am aware of the fact that these bids are binding. (The cars will be sold in the fashion stated in the memo distributed after the information meeting on May 24.) I understand that the highest bidder will get the car that is auctioned off – if not this person has obtained a car in an earlier round and therefore been eliminated from further participation. I hereby declare that, if the highest bidder, I will make a downpayment of SEK 1,000 and complete the purchase on May 30, at the latest.

Signature
NOTE THAT THE TEXT MAY NOT BE ALTERED"

Appendix C Information, Presenting the Main Points of the Instructions in Writing, Distributed at the End of the Information Meeting

A selection:

"....
2. You will get two forms to complete. The *light-green* one looks like this: /See the first part of Appendix B for text inserted here/
The *white* one looks like this: /Appendix B, second part!/
3. We want you to complete both forms, sign and state your name in block letters. Check your statements carefully!

Remember

a) that you cannot get more than one car; the reason is that the person who gets the first car will be left out from the auction of the second car. Thus, you can state your highest price for both cars knowing that you will get, at most, one.

b) that, when stating your bids, you may want to consider two ways in which you could use a car: keep it, of course, or resell it right away.
c) that your bids will have to be stated in even SEK 100s; we will reduce uneven bids to the nearest SEK 100 figure.
d) that the bid you state for each car determines (1) whether you get the car (the highest bidder gets it) and (2) the *amount* you receive *if* you win the lottery and *if* the car you win must be auctioned off (determined by tossing a coin) and *if* someone other than you has the highest bid on this car; since your bid thus has two potential "roles" to play, it seems appropriate to suggest that you carefully consider your bids.
e) that it is also important to consider carefully the order in which you want to rank the cars, since this order determines what car you are most likely to get – or receive money for – in case you win the lottery.

4. After completing the forms, you return them to us. On your way back to your seat please check that your number is among the lottery "tickets" on the table up front.
5. The lottery takes place. The person whose number comes up will now have to wait until it is determined by a draw which car the prize relates to: There is a 2/3 chance of getting the car the winner has said he or she prefers, 1/3 chance for the other one. (In case the winner has stated that the cars are equally good, we toss a coin to get the prize car.)
6. Now, we have the prize car! We toss a coin to see whether the winner gets the car or the money he or she has bid on this car. Heads for the car, tails for the money. Thus, if heads, the car is "lost" to the winner and won't be auctioned off.
7. If tails, there will be an auction on this car. The highest bidder gets the car at a *price equal to that of the second highest bidder*. You should take this into account when stating your bids – that you never have to pay the price of your bid, only the *lower* price equal to that of second highest bid. In addition, please note that

i) if the winner, whose prize car is to be auctioned off, also happens to be the highest bidder on this car, he or she simply gets the car for keeps.
ii) if there are *two or more persons stating the same highest bid* on a car, lottery will be arranged among them to select a winner; the winner pays the highest price *below* that stated by the winner.

8. The winner pays a down payment of SEK 1,000 and enters an agreement with us, stating when – Tuesday May 30, at the latest – the purchase will be completed and the car picked up.
9. The remaining car is auctioned off. The bid from the person who got the first car is excluded. The highest bidder among those remaining wins this second car and pays the second highest price. Payment and car delivery as explained in the preceding point.

PLEASE ... Don't forget to bring enough money on Monday! Look forward to seeing you!
Staffan Stockeld /in charge of the administration of the experiment/
..."

References

Becker G, DeGroot M, Marshak J (1964) Measuring utility by a single response sequential method. Behavioral Science 9:226–32
Cox J, Epstein S (1989) Preference reversals without the independence axiom. American Economic Review 79:408–26
Grether D, Plott C (1979) Economic theory of choice and the preference reversal phenomenon. American Economic Review 69:623–38
Harrison G (1989) Expected utility theory and the experimentalists. Working Paper, University of New Mexico
Holt C (1986) Preference reversals and the independence axiom. American Economic Review 76: 508–14
Karni E, Safra Z (1987) Preference reversals and the observability of preferences by experimental methods. Econometrica 55:675–85
Lichentenstien S, Slovic P (1971) Reversals of preference between bids and choices in gambling decisions. Journal of Experimental Psychology 89:46–55
Loomes G, Sugden R (1983) A rationale for preference reversal. American Economic Review 73: 428–32
Loomes G, Starmer C, Sugden R (1989) Preference reversal: Information-processing effect or rational non-transitive choice?. Economic Journal 99:140–51
Machina M (1987) Choice under uncertainty: Problems solved and unsolved. Journal of Economic Perspectives 1:121–54
Pommerehne W, Schneider F, Zweifel P (1982) Economic theory of choice and the preference reversal phenomenon: A reexamination. American Economic Review 72:569–74
Reilly R (1982) Preference reversal: Further evidence and some suggested modifications in experimental design. American Economic Review
Segal U (1988) Does the preference reversal phenomenon necessarily contradict the independence axiom. American Economic Review 78:233–36
Slovic P, Lichenstein S (1983) Preference reversals: A broader perspective. American Economic Review 73:596–605
Smith V (1982) Microeconomic systems as an experimental science. American Economic Review 72:923–55
Vickrey (1961) Counterspeculation, auctions, and competitive sealed tenders. Journal of Finance 16:181–201

The Impact of Fairness on Bargaining Behaviour

PAUL BURROWS AND GRAHAM LOOMES[1]

Centre for Experimental Economics, University of York, York, YOI SDD, United Kingdom

Abstract: A number of bargaining experiments have raised the possibility that individuals' notions of what is fair or just may be sufficiently powerful to generate behaviour which departs substantially and systematically from the predictions of standard bargaining models. This paper reports an experiment designed to test whether the relative impact of different notions of fairness varies with certain changes in the bargaining environment.

JEL-Classification System-Numbers: C71, C92, D63

1 The Influence of Fairness on Behaviour

1.1 Fairness, Markets and Bargains

It is increasingly accepted by economists that people's notions of fairness can act as a moderating influence on their pursuit of self interest (see, for example, Kahneman et al (1986) on impersonal market situations, Hoffman and Spitzer (1982, 1985), Thaler (1988) and Ochs and Roth (1989) on bargaining). In the impersonal market context many people appear to regard as unfair attempts to take advantage of abnormal conditions at other people's expense: hence the hostility to price rises in times of unusually acute shortages. However, the anonymity of the agents in many markets obscures any issue of distributive justice beyond a general dislike of opportunism in conditions of adversity.

In direct bargaining situations, on the other hand, the participants' knowledge of each other is sometimes greater, so one might expect that here fairness would have a closer connection with ideas of distributive justice. But there is no reason to expect that any influence of fairness on behaviour will be uniform across different bargaining contexts. Hoffman and Spitzer suggested that peo-

[1] Funding for the experimental work in this paper was provided by the Economic and Social Research Council, Award No. R000231194. We should like to thank Helen Hawksby for her help with preparing the materials, and David Ansic and Karl Claxton for their assistance with processing the data. Graham Loomes gratefully acknowledges the support of the Nuffield Foundation in the form of a Social Science Research Fellowship.

ple's inclination to go for the equal splitting of final joint payoffs[2], which the authors attributed to egalitarian attitudes, is the greater under the following conditions:

- repeated, face-to-face negotiations
- bargainers have the option of a Pareto optimal allocation that involves an equal split
- payoffs are made in public
- each bargainer has full information about the other parties.

It should come as no surprise, therefore, if the results of the empirical tests of the degree of influence of fairness on behaviour depend very much on the *nature* of the bargaining situations being studied (Thaler's analysis, (1988, p.205), implies as much. See also Ochs and Roth (1989, p.379)). A plausible extension of this argument is that the *particular notion* of fairness that dominates may depend on the bargaining situation as well.

In this paper, we shall be primarily concerned with one aspect of the bargaining environment, namely the origins of the initial entitlements from which bargaining can commence. Hoffman and Spitzer (1985, p.260) have hypothesised, for example, that people do not regard pure chance as a just way of allocating unequal entitlements. This could account for the willingness of bargainers to offset random differences in payoff opportunities by the equal splitting of final payoff sums, rather than settling for, say, equal shares of the gains from a bargain in excess of a non-cooperative outcome, which would have left the parties' final payoffs unequal. In some cases bargainers in their experiments went so far as to agree to an equal split of the final joint payoff even when this meant that the value of their own final sum was *less* than they could have achieved from their best non-cooperative outcome.

These results provide the starting point for our analysis. In section 2 we will outline the Hoffman and Spitzer results, and explain the misgivings about their experimental design which motivated our own experiment. But first, we briefly review the notions of fairness which the tests are concerned with.

1.2 Notions of Fairness

The experiments conducted by Hoffman and Spitzer, and our experiment as well, are intended to discriminate between three attitudes:

[2] Final joint payoff is defined as the sum of the two parties' entitlements at the end of a transaction (usually in an experimental context) relative to the status quo ante which is a zero entitlement each. This is larger than the joint *bargaining* gain which is the difference between the sum of the two parties' entitlements in a non-cooperative outcome and the sum after a bargain is reached.

1) *utilitarian*: this is interpreted as implying self-regarding behaviour (no interdependence of utility functions), which means that a person will maximise his own return either by a unilateral choice of a non-cooperative outcome or by restricting his acceptance of bargains to those in which he is no worse off than with his best non-cooperative outcome. This extreme form of utilitarianism has dubious status as a notion of fairness (Veljanovski (1981)), but it does provide a basis of comparison for the other two theories.
2) *egalitarian*: interpreted as requiring the equal splitting of the final payoff sum regardless of how the payoff options, or entitlements, of each of the parties were determined.
3) *desert*: Hoffman and Spitzer adopted what they regarded as a Lockean notion of an entitlement to resources which have been produced through the person's expenditure of effort. Differentials in payoffs are deserved, and are therefore fair, if they correlate positively with the amount of effort involved in obtaining them. This view can be presented in a way that makes it clear that people's adherence to a feeling that others are deserving is likely to be highly context-specific.

Rawls (1971) argued that a person could be said to deserve the fruits of his actions only to the extent that he deserves the conditions which makes his action possible. On this argument one does not deserve the entire fruits of one's ability because ability antedates action and cannot be said to be deserved. Sher (1987, p.16) has responded to this strict interpretation, which effectively rules out any realistic basis of desert claim, by favouring the alternative view that a person can deserve the benefits of his action only if he deserves those conditions of the action *which are not shared by* his rivals. For then he is *relatively* deserving. One of Sher's claims is that the ability to make an *effort* is not sufficiently unequally distributed across individuals to make it impossible for different people to exert a similar level of effort. On this argument differences in effort provide one basis for desert claims, since such differences cannot be attributed entirely to an undeserved necessary condition for the effort. This view may not be unchallengeable, but it does suggest that effort may provide one, but not the only, basis of desert claims which will find some measure of popular support. Sher's analysis of diligence and desert (1987, ch.4) centres on the proposition that sustained effort is an investment of oneself, and therefore confers more value than does simply desiring something, as long as the effort does not harm others. But clearly this rationalisation of desert claims will hold *only* for contexts in which everyone has the same ability and opportunity to make an effort and the rewards are clearly linked to the degree of effort made. One aim of our experiment is to test whether, under conditions approximating such equality, people behave *as if* effort were socially recognised as a basis of a relative desert claim.

2 Hoffman and Spitzer's (1985) Experiment

2.1 Design and Results

That experiment involved eighty six students and staff members at two U.S. universities in two-person face-to-face bargaining situations. Both participants in each case were fully informed of the other's payoff. The procedure in each case was to tell the pair that they were about to make two decisions concerning the payoffs to be received in cash by each party at the end of the experiment. The choice of payoffs is to be made by a 'controller' who, in the absence of a bargain to the contrary, can unilaterally choose the payoff for *both* parties by selecting one of the seven payoff options shown in Table 1.

Each pair faces this situation and then a repeat decision with a slightly different payoff structure. For each pair the person who is to be the controller is decided either by a toss of a coin or by who wins a simple hash mark game.[3] Notice that the controller alone determines the payoff for the loser, unless the loser can arrive at a bargain with the winner concerning the number from the payoff sheet to be chosen, so the loser has no independent entitlement in either the coin toss or the hash game situation. Half of the trials used the hash game and half the toss of a coin.

Hoffman and Spitzer added another element to the bargaining situation. In one half of the coin toss cases and in one half of the hash game cases, the controller was told that he had *earned* the entitlement which his position as controller gave him; in the other half he was told simply that he had been *designated* the controller as a result of winning the coin toss or the hash game. This was to test for the effect of the experiment organiser's moral authority. This 2 × 2 categorisation meant that there were four 'treatments' (left hand column

Table 1. Hoffman and Spitzer's first set of payoffs

Number	*A*'s Payoff	*B*'s Payoff
1	$ 0.00	$ 12.00
2	4.00	10.00
3	6.00	6.00
4	7.50	4.00
5	9.00	2.50
6	10.50	1.00
7	12.00	0.00

[3] The hash game is on a par with noughts and crosses. Each person in turn crosses out one, two, three or four of seventeen hash marks. The person who crosses out the last hash mark is the loser. Each pair plays the game twice, taking turns to go first.

Table 2. Hoffman and Spitzer's summary of results

Experiment	Number of Decisions (N)	Number of Joint Maxima (N_1)	Equal Split (N_2)	Equal ±$ 1.00 (N_3)	Controller Receives his Maximum (N_4)	Controller Receives more than Maximum (N_5)	Halfway between Equal and Controller Max. (N_6)	Other (N_7)
A. Coin flip:								
1. No moral authority	22	20	10	4	3	3	2	0
2. Moral authority	20	19	9	1	5	1	2	2
B. Game trigger:								
1. No moral authority	22	18	9	4	2	4	3	0
2. Moral authority	22	21	4	3	3	12	0	0
Total	86	78	32	12	13	20	7	2

of Table 2) with no more than 22 observations in each of the categories. No participant experienced more than one of the four treatments.

The coin toss is used to represent luck in obtaining initial entitlements, and the hash game to represent effort. The moral authority/no moral authority distinction is superimposed on the luck/effort comparison, although it does not seem to relate directly to the main comparison between notions of fairness except in as far as moral authority may reinforce people's judgement as to whether an initial entitlement has been earned.

In Table 2 we reproduce the summary of results (Hoffman and Spitzer's Table 1, p. 276). On the basis of these results and some associated significance tests and ancillary results, Hoffman and Spitzer offer an interpretation of the participants' behaviour. First they point to the fact that in 91% of cases the pairs arrived at the outcome which maximised the joint final payoff (number 2 on the payoff sheet in Table 1). Then comes a comparison of the proportion of cases in which the joint final payoff was nearly split equally (equal ± $1.00):

61% in all the experiments with no moral authority
40% in the presence of such authority
32% in the experiments with both moral authority *and* the hash game operating (68% in this case gave the controller at least his non-cooperative outcome). The percentage fell from 50% to 32% when the coin toss was replaced by the hash game in the presence of moral authority, but only from 64% to 59% when moral authority was absent.

The average excess of the controller's share over an equal share increased when the hash game replaced the coin toss (aggregating the with and without moral authority experiments) but the hash game effect was only weakly significant; on the other hand, replacing no moral authority with moral authority (aggregating the coin toss and hash game experiments) had a stronger positive effect on the controllers' shares.

The conclusion offered by Hoffman and Spitzer is that people behaved as if they believed in desert rather than as utilitarians or egalitarians "except where there was no morally relevant distinction between themselves, at which time they fell back to egalitarian norms" (1985, p.283). A similar conclusion was reached by Güth (1988, p.707).

2.2 *Misgivings*

Hoffman and Spitzer's 1985 experiments are interesting because they yield information about:

a) people's inclination to direct their bargaining towards outcomes that maximise joint payoffs.

and

b) the effect that factors other than the payoff structure have on the division of the amounts available.

However, we have certain reservations about the design of the experiments and the interpretation of the data. These, together with a desire to extend the analysis somewhat, motivated the new experiment described in subsequent sections.

First, our main misgivings. In any experiment of this kind, a key issue is the ability of the design to discriminate effectively between the competing hypotheses. In the present case, where three different notions of distributive justice are being considered, we ideally require an experimental design which allows all three to manifest themselves in distinctive patterns of behaviour. Consider this in relation to Table 2. Egalitarian behaviour, as defined by Hoffman and Spitzer, entails a nearly equal split irrespective of treatment, i.e. columns N_2 and N_3 in the table. Utilitarian behaviour requires an agent "to enter only into bargains that he believes will leave him no worse off than if he had not traded at all" (p.263). This would involve controllers receiving at least their non-cooperative maximum i.e. columns N_4 and N_5.

Does this mean that 'desert' is manifested only in the other columns, N_6 and N_7? If it does, Hoffman and Spitzer's interpretation of their data appears to be questionable. By their argument, the hash game provides a basis for desert whereas the coin flip does not. Yet even without the game trigger there are 6 observations in rows A1 and A2 that fall into categories N_6 and N_7, while the introduction of the hash game does not increase this figure. Even though there are more observations in rows B1 and B2, the number falling into categories N_6 and N_7 is only 3. In fact, as an inspection of Table 2 shows, the only really significant change occurs when the game trigger is reinforced by moral authority – and this has the effect of shifting observations from N_2 (egalitarian) to N_5 (utilitarian). Viewed in this way, desert does not appear to offer a very powerful account of the data.

Hoffman and Spitzer's interpretation could perhaps be sustained if it could be argued that desert was liable to manifest itself in the difference between the frequency of $N_4 + N_5$ with the game trigger and the frequency of $N_4 + N_5$ with the coin flip. However, the difference here *does not arise in the absence of moral authority*: by itself, skill and/or effort, as reflected by the hash game, make no impact on the number of observations in $N_4 + N_5$. It is only when moral authority is combined with the game trigger that any substantial effect is observed in Table 2; but whether this is because the subjects' attention has been drawn to the idea that they might be thought deserving, or because the experimenters' authority has legitimised utilitarian 'greed', is a question which cannot be answered within the terms of Hoffman and Spitzer's experiment.

Nevertheless some further consideration of the question may be productive. Suppose a pair of individuals behave like Lockeans, as defined by Hoffman and Spitzer. How should we expect them to react in the hash game situations? In principle, the experimenters' form of words should make no difference unless the wording affects the individuals' perceptions of the *relative* inputs of effort put in by the players of the hash game. We have no means of observing this in Hoffman and Spitzer's design, since all we can observe in each case is that one person wins and the other loses.

However, any pair of subjects may each form some view about the amount of effort expended by themselves and by their opponent. If they behave like Lockeans, and if there were some objective, mutually acceptable and/or salient measure of effort, we might expect them to maximise joint payoffs and divide the total according to the ratio revealed by that measure. In the absence of any such measure, the perceived relative amounts of effort that have been put in becomes the prime object of negotiation: if they can reach an agreement on this ratio, they should maximise joint payoffs and divide the total according to that ratio; if they cannot agree, the controller has the option of taking his $12.00 and dividing it according to his perception of relative inputs. But in either case, it seems unlikely that the ratio of relative effort will be judged to be as high or higher than 12:2 (the minimum necessary to produce desert-based observations in N_4 or N_5). Our conclusion is that Hoffman and Spitzer's experimental results cannot be regarded as providing convincing support for their conclusion quoted at the end of section 2.1 above.

The problem of arriving at any firm conclusion is intensified by the rather small sample size, which means that even though subjects were randomised between treatments, there were only 10 or 11 pairs in each treatment cell. Each subject bargained only twice – both times with the same person – so that we have no real information about any *learning*, or about individuals' sequential interactions with a number of others; nor do we have any indication of how the same individual's behaviour might be affected by the different treatment variables. In addition we have some reservations about the interpretation of success in the hash games as an indicator of effort and therefore as a basis of desert claim. For one thing, the either/or (win/lose) nature of the outcome means that it cannot relate to the *degree* of effort put in by the two players. This is the inevitable consequence of designing the experiment so that there is a competition for the position of controller. A second problematic feature of the hash game outcome as an indicator of effort is that the game has an unbeatable strategy for the person who plays first. Anyone who knows the strategy in advance will need to exert no effort to win when playing first, and anyone who doesn't already know it is unlikely to discover the strategy without repeated games. Winning the hash game seems, therefore, just as likely to be attributed to good luck as to effort[4]. These two problematic aspects of the hash game cast doubt on its suitability as a context for relative desert claims as described in section 1.2.

[4] Although Hoffman and Spitzer (1985, pp. 273–4) go to some lengths to deny this.

3 A New Experiment to Test Notions of Fairness

3.1 The Broad Structure

We developed our experimental design in the light of our concerns discussed above, and in order to investigate other issues such as the impact of different 'treatments' on the same individuals. Our design is described in detail in the next subsection, but it may be helpful here to outline the key features.

The experiment was conducted in two stages, henceforth Stage 1 and Stage 2. In Stage 1, initial endowments were decided randomly, whereas in Stage 2 they were based on performance in a piecerate work task. We avoided any additional moral authority/no moral authority distinction, preferring to focus attention entirely on the impact of the change in the allocative mechanism. Moreover, since all subjects in Stage 2 had participated in Stage 1, we could examine the extent of any impact on each individual.

In Hoffman and Spitzer's experiment, it is not absolutely clear how subjects perceived the position at the time they started bargaining. Hoffman and Spitzer implicitly assume that after the coin flip/hash game has determined who is the controller, both parties act as if they are starting from a $12:0 distribution i.e. from the non-cooperative payoffs which the controller has the right to impose. Relative to this, the gains from bargaining are small – just $2, if subjects agree to maximise joint payoffs. However, the $12:0 distribution is not actually imposed by the experimenter. Although conventional economic theory might not make any distinction, we were concerned that there may be a psychological difference between starting to bargain from a position where a $12:0 distribution has been imposed by the experimenter, compared with the position where both parties as yet have no actual money allocation, but one of the two has an entitlement which only becomes a $12:0 distribution if he chooses to invoke it in that way.

To avoid any such difficulty, we opted for a design where there is no ambiguity about the position from which bargaining begins. Moreover, our experiment offers larger potential gains from bargaining, which range from £2.00 to £12.50 in Stage 1, and could be as high as £18.00 in Stage 2, giving a good deal more room for different bargaining approaches to manifest themselves in distinctive ways of dividing up the total sums achieved.

Finally in both Stages each subject took part in a series of up to nine bilateral bargains, each time with a different person. This was intended to allow us to observe any learning effects that might occur.

To see how these broad design objectives were implemented, we now give a more detailed description.

3.2 The Experimental Design in Detail

Stage 1 comprised 12 sessions, each involving up to a maximum of 10 subjects. In some sessions, fewer than 10 subjects attended, so that the total number of participants in Stage 1 was 104, recruited by open invitation from among the undergraduate and graduate population at the University of York.

On signing up to participate in a particular session, people were given two pages of information describing the Stage 1 experimental design, which they were asked to read and think about before coming to their session. This was intended to give subjects an opportunity to consider possible strategies beforehand. In addition, each session began with a practice period, at the end of which subjects were invited to ask for any clarification they might require.

The number of rounds of bargaining in any session depended on how many subjects attended: each session consisted of sufficient rounds for each subject to be paired once and only once with every other subject. Each subject was given a Record Sheet on which all relevant information was recorded, and they were reminded that at the end of the session just one round would be selected at random (by rolling a die) and that everyone would be paid on the basis of that one round.

At the beginning of a round, both people in each pair drew a card, one from a red pack, the other from a blue pack. These cards gave each person their initial endowment in the form of Black and White tokens in various quantities and with various ratios of values.

Table 3 describes all the possible initial endowments. This information was included in the details circulated in advance. There were 24 cards in each pack, three cards for each of the endowments R1-R8 and B1-B8.

As an example of the procedure, consider a pair where the person drawing from the red pack picks R7 – 20 Black tokens each worth 15p to him plus 40 White tokens each worth 5p, giving an initial endowment worth £5.00 – while the person drawing from the blue pack picks B5 – 30 Blacks worth 5p each plus 10 Whites each worth 10p, making a total starting value of £2.50.

Both cards are placed face up. Each subject copies the details of their own endowment onto their Record Sheet, then records the details of the other's initial endowment.

The two pack system ensures that the ratio of values of Black and White tokens must differ between any pair of subjects, so that there will always be potential gains from bargaining. Neither side is obliged to enter into a deal: if they do not reach any other agreement, both subjects stand to receive their initial endowment, should that round happen to be selected as the basis for payment. However, the precirculated details draw attention to the possibility of gains from bargaining, in the following words:

"Alternatively, you and the other person could agree to do some deal which would make one or both of you better off. There are any number of deals you *could* do – what you actually do is *entirely up to you and the other person to sort out between you.* However, most deals are likely to take one of two forms:

Table 3. The values on the cards in each pack

Red pack	Starting value	BLACK : WHITE value ratio
R1: 10 BLACK @ 20p + 10 WHITE @ 5p	£2.50	
R2: 15 " " + 15 " "	£3.75	
R3: 20 " " + 20 " "	£5.00	4 : 1
R4: 25 " " + 25 " "	£6.25	
R5: 10 BLACK @ 15p + 20 WHITE @ 5p	£2.50	
R6: 15 " " + 30 " "	£3.75	
R7: 20 " " + 40 " "	£5.00	3 : 1
R8: 25 " " + 50 " "	£6.25	
Blue pack		
B1: 20 BLACK @ 5p + 30 WHITE @ 5p	£2.50	
B2: 30 " " + 45 " "	£3.75	
B3: 40 " " + 60 " "	£5.00	1 : 1
B4: 50 " " + 75 " "	£6.25	
B5: 30 BLACK @ 5p + 10 WHITE @ 10p	£2.50	
B6: 45 " " + 15 " "	£3.75	
B7: 60 " " + 20 " "	£5.00	1 : 2
B8: 75 " " + 25 " "	£6.25	

i) A *trade*, where the two of you agree to exchange some number of BLACK tokens for some number of WHITES.
ii) a *contract* (in writing), where either person may take some or all of the other person's tokens in return for agreeing to pay some amount of money if this round turns out to be the one on which payment is based.

Here are examples of (i) and (ii). They are just to illustrate the points – they are not necessarily what any two people would or should agree to do.

Example of (i): Recall that you start with 20 BLACKS each worth 15p to you and 40 WHITES each worth 5p to you, total value £5, ratio 3:1. S/he starts with 30 BLACKS (5p each) and 10 WHITES (10p each), total value £2.50, ratio 1:2. If you gave 20 WHITES and got 10 BLACKS in exchange, you would end up with 30 BLACKS and 20 WHITES, and the other person would end up with 20 BLACKS and 30 WHITES. If that round were chosen to be the basis of your payments, you would get £5.50 (30 BLACKS @ 15p + 20 WHITES @ 5p) and the other person would get £4.00 (20 @ 5p + 30 @ 10p). So you would both end up with more than if you hadn't traded.
Example of (ii): You both start as before, but instead of a direct exchange, you give the other person all 40 of your WHITES in return for a written promise that s/he will pay you £3 if the round is chosen for payment. If it is, the other person will cash in 30 BLACKS @ 5p + 50 WHITES @ 10p for a total of £6.50. Out of that, s/he will pay you £3, to which you add £3 from cashing in your 20

BLACKS @ 15p each. So you end up with £6 and the other person with £3.50 – again, you are both better off than you started."

Care was taken to provide examples where final payoffs were not equal, and where the particular sidepayment solution did not give both people higher payoffs than simple trading. Contract forms were provided routinely, along with rough paper for any calculations, on every table in the room. Our intention was to avoid suggesting that any particular way of proceeding was expected: part of the objective of the experiment was to see whether subjects would work out in advance how to maximise joint payoffs, or whether (and how rapidly) they would learn by experience and interaction. And obviously we wanted to avoid any suggestion of how the total payoff should be divided between any two people.

Once all subjects had drawn their cards and copied the relevant information onto their Record Sheets, the bargaining period began: there was a time limit of 5 minutes, although most deals were completed well within that time. Details of any deal was recorded by both members of a pair on their Record Sheets, with each person signing the other's sheet as being a correct record, as well as both people signing any contract they had drawn up between them.

At the end of each round, any contracts were collected, and all cards were replaced in their packs. Subjects then formed fresh pairs, and a new round began, with each subject drawing afresh from the appropriate pack of cards. Thus the same procedure was repeated in each round, until every subject had been paired with every other subject. At this point, a round was selected at random, Record Sheets and any contracts were consulted, and subjects were paid accordingly (with the organisers enforcing any contracts).

At the time of signing up, subjects had been told that there would be a second session, different from and independent of the first, but they were not given any information about the follow-up sessions until Stage 1 had been completed. Then details were circulated to all those who had participated in Stage 1 and they were invited to sign up as before.

In actual fact, there were two types of follow-up experiment, and although subjects had details of both types in advance, they did not know which type they would be taking part in until they arrived at the beginning of the session. Some follow-up sessions were concerned with bargaining between groups of three or four people, compared with the pairwise bargaining in Stage 1 – but these results will not be discussed in the present paper. Here we focus on the other type of session, designed to look at issues raised by Hoffman and Spitzer's experiment.

In most respects these sessions operated in the same way as Stage 1 i.e. pairwise face-to-face bargaining with each subject meeting every other subject once, and with one round being selected as the basis for payment, etc.

However, the key difference was that in Stage 2, initial endowments were *not* allocated at random. Instead, at the beginning of each session, subjects were presented with a task by means of which they earned the value of their initial

YOUR NAME ______________________

36 words, listed below in alphabetical order, are hidden in the square underneath. Some are written forwards, some backwards, upwards, downwards, or even diagonally. They are all 6 letters long. Find as many as you can in the time allowed, and mark each one you find by drawing a *single straight red line* through it. As examples, four other words have already been marked: DENOTE, HANDLE, MASTER and TUSSLE.

You will be paid strictly in proportion to the number of words you find in the time. These are the 36 words which are hidden:

ACTION	CREASE	EXPECT	LESSON	PREACH	STREAM
AMOUNT	DEEPER	FLOWER	MOBILE	REMOVE	TACKLE
AROUSE	DESIRE	GARBLE	NARROW	REVEAL	THROWN
BLEACH	EFFECT	GREASE	NATURE	SCORCH	UPSHOT
COPIED	ESTATE	HONEST	OPPOSE	SOOTHE	VALLEY
CRADLE	EXCEPT	KNIGHT	PLANET	SPEECH	WINDOW

E	L	D	N	A	H	A	H	C	A	E	L	B	E	P
H	C	R	O	C	S	R	P	U	X	E	L	D	L	B
R	R	T	I	C	Y	S	D	C	L	S	K	A	K	E
E	A	O	T	H	O	N	E	S	T	A	N	G	C	K
T	D	H	C	E	E	P	S	L	C	E	I	V	A	R
S	L	S	A	O	T	U	I	A	T	R	G	A	T	E
A	E	P	D	P	T	P	R	E	A	C	H	L	W	L
M	D	U	T	P	H	O	E	V	D	S	T	L	G	I
A	E	A	M	O	U	N	T	E	V	O	M	E	R	B
E	N	O	S	S	E	L	E	R	S	O	F	Y	E	O
R	O	A	E	E	M	P	J	F	S	T	R	E	A	M
U	T	O	R	R	E	W	O	L	F	H	A	I	S	H
T	E	L	B	R	A	G	E	X	P	E	C	T	E	B
A	W	I	N	D	O	W	G	M	V	A	C	F	E	R
N	U	P	N	C	N	W	O	R	H	T	E	T	I	L

Fig. 1

endowment. That task is reproduced in Figure 1. Subjects were given 8 minutes to find as many of the words as they could, each word found being worth 25p. Then their sheets were checked, and the number of words found, together with the total value of their starting endowment, was written in red on their Record Sheets.

Then the first round began. As before, one person in a pair chose a red card, the other a blue card; however, this time the purpose was not to determine starting values – that had already been decided by their word score – but simply to determine the proportions of Black and White tokens and the ratio of their values. For example, consider the case of someone who has found 31 words, worth £7.75, and who then draws B5. He gets 3 Black tokens (worth 5p each) and 1 White token (worth 10p) for every word found – hence he starts with 93

Black and 31 White tokens. Someone who identified 17 words and drew R3 would start the round with 17 Black (20p each) and 17 White (5p each) giving an initial endowment value of £4.25.

Then, as in Stage 1, both people would write all these details on their Record Sheets; bargaining followed, just as in Stage 1; and when the time limit expired, details of agreements were recorded, contracts collected, and cards replaced in their packs, all as in Stage 1, before subjects formed fresh pairs and moved into the next round. Altogether, 6 sessions of this type were run, involving a total of 47 subjects, all of whom had, of course, participated in Stage 1.

4 Results and Interpretation

We begin by considering what patterns of behaviour would be consistent with the three typologies – utilitarian, egalitarian and desert – and how the data might allow us to distinguish between them.

The behaviour implied by egalitarianism is most straightforward to define: subjects will attempt to maximise joint payoffs, and then divide the total equally, irrespective of the distribution of initial endowments; and this behaviour should hold equally for Stage 1 and Stage 2.

Utilitarians can be expected to maximise the final joint payoffs and divide these totals so that neither party is made worse off by the bargain. Any solution that meets these criteria satisfies Pareto optimality. We might think that the most salient of all Pareto optimal solutions would be to divide the *gains* from bargaining equally, although we cannot insist that this is the *only* pattern consistent with utilitarianism. But there is no need to make such a restrictive prediction: all we really require is that the overall pattern of behaviour should not change from Stage 1 to Stage 2, but should satisfy the Paretian criteria and be significantly different from the pattern entailed by egalitarianism.

Whereas utilitarian and egalitarian behaviour should not be influenced by the differences between the Stage 1 and Stage 2 environments, considerations of desert *can* be expected to induce a change in behaviour. In Stage 1, where there is no effort involved in determining initial endowments, both sides are equally deserving, and one might expect 50–50 splitting of the maximised total payoffs: that is, in Stage 1, desert and egalitarian behaviour should coincide. However in Stage 2, one interpretation of the notion of desert would entail outputs (final payments) being correlated with inputs (and, by implication, with the endowments earned during the work task) so that the division of the maximised total payoff would correspond with the ratio of endowments, assuming that subjects take wordscores to be an acceptable proxy for relative effort. This correlation of outputs and inputs corresponds to Güth's 'observable work standard' of equity (Güth 1988, p.707), and it usually implies a widening of the absolute difference between a pair's payoffs due to the unequal sharing of bargaining gains.

We organised the data from each Stage into six categories. We shall first define each of these categories and then discuss how they related to the various notions of fairness being considered.

C_1: Cases where the value of initial endowments was the same for both bargainers. (In such cases, all three notions of fairness are consistent with dividing the total equally, so that observations in this category cannot help us to discriminate between the different notions. For our purposes, it is all the other cases, where bargainers begin with unequal initial endowments, which are potentially most telling.)

C_2: Cases where initial endowments were unequal, but where the final total was divided equally. (Because some totals involved odd numbers of pence, and because there was some evidence of rounding, we regard any difference of 25p or less as being equal for the purpose of categorisation.)

C_3: Cases where the gains from trade were split equally, thus maintaining the difference between the values of initial endowments.

C_4: Cases where the gains from trade were divided unequally, in such a way as to *partially* offset differences between initial endowments.

C_5: Cases where the gains from trade were divided unequally, in such a way as to make the difference between final payoffs *greater* than the difference between initial endowments.

C_6: Cases where the unequal division of gains from trade *more than offset* the initial difference i.e. the subject who began with the less valuable endowment actually ended up with a payoff more than 25p greater than the other subject's final payoff.

Before considering the relative frequencies of these categories in each of the two Stages, let us formulate our hypotheses in terms of the categories defined above and be clear about what we are – and what we are *not* – attempting to test in this experiment.

From earlier work by other researchers we have taken three characterisations of how subjects *might* behave in face-to-face pairwise bargaining situations. We are not suggesting that these are the *only* ways of characterising bargaining behavior. And we are *certainly not* restricting ourselves to testing the hypothesis that all subjects behave in the same way. We allow for the possibility that our sample may be composed of individuals who have different attitudes towards fairness.

If our sample were to consist only of utilitarians, or egalitarians, or some mixture of the two, we should expect the difference between Stage 1 and Stage 2 to have no systematic effect on the relative frequencies of C_2 to C_6. We take this as our null hypothesis.

On the other hand, if our sample were to include a substantial number of individuals who subscribe to the desert notion as defined earlier, we should expect to see a shift from C_2 to C_5 as we go from Stage 1 to Stage 2. We might regard this as the alternative hypothesis consistent with Hoffman and Spitzer's interpretation of their 1982 and 1985 experiments.

Table 4. Frequencies of bargaining categories

Stage 1

Group	No. of Pairs	Equal initial endowment (equal final payoffs) C_1	Unequal initial endowments: Equal final payoffs C_2	Equal split of gains C_3	Gains unequally split but equalising C_4	Gains unequally split and widening differences C_5	Gains unequally split reversing initial differences C_6
1.1	21	7(6)	6	5	1	1	1
1.2	28	6(6)	6	8	4	4	0
1.3	36	2(2)	16	5	6	4	3
1.4	45	13(13)	27	2	1	1	1
1.5	45	12(11)	11	13	7	1	1
1.6	45	10(10)	29	4	2	0	0
1.7	45	11(10)	7	16	6	3	2
1.8	45	9(9)	32	0	3	0	1
1.9	21	8(7)	7	0	3	1	2
1.10	15	4(3)	8	0	1	1	1
1.11	21	6(4)	4	1	6	3	1
1.12	45	15(14)	15	9	2	2	2
Total	412	103(95)	168	63	42	21	15
Percentage of C_2 to C_6			54.4	20.4	13.6	6.8	4.8

Stage 2

Group	No. of Pairs	C_1	C_2	C_3	C_4	C_5	C_6
2.1	45	1(1)	12	29	1	1	1
2.2	36	2(2)	3	21	5	5	0
2.3	36	1(1)	1	21	6	5	2
2.4	21	1(1)	8	4	5	3	0
2.5	6	0(0)	2	2	0	2	0
2.6	28	1(1)	13	12	1	1	0
Total	172	6(6)	39	89	18	17	3
Percentage of C_2 to C_6			23.5	53.6	10.8	10.2	1.8

Before considering how far these hypotheses are consistent with the results of the present experiment, several points are worth noting. First, comparing the pattern of Stage 1 results for those who also participated in Stage 2 with the pattern for those who did *not* take part in Stage 2, we found no significant difference. In what follows, therefore, we shall use all the data from both Stages. The data are organised into categories C_1 to C_6 in Table 4.

The second point refers to something which cannot be adduced from Table 4, namely the success with which subjects extracted the maximum possible joint payoff. Out of 412 negotiations in Stage 1, there were only 15 cases where a pair of subjects earned less than they might have done; and in Stage 2 there were only 4 such cases out of a total of 172 pairwise negotiations. This is encouraging, since it suggests that the great majority of participants had understood the essential mechanics of the experiment.

The third point refers to the C_1 category in Table 4. Numbers in brackets indicate the cases where the total was divided equally between the two bargainers. As expected this accounted for the overwhelming majority of cases in this category.

So, as indicated earlier, we shall set aside the C_1 observations and concentrate on the relative frequencies of C_2 to C_6. It is immediately clear from Table 4 that we can confidently reject the null hypothesis that there is no significant difference between the two distributions ($\chi^2 = 65.77$, 4 d.f.) However, the evidence can hardly be said to support the alternative hypothesis. The frequency of C_5 did increase a little in Stage 2, but the main difference was an increase in C_3 of sufficient magnitude that the relative frequencies of C_2 and C_3 were virtually transposed[5]. So there is a clear effect here, but it is one which does not fit easily with a view of our sample as containing some mixture of utilitarians, egalitarians and 'Lockeans' as defined in section 1.2

Still, such a marked effect requires a further attempt at explanation. In the remainder of this section we shall explore two other possible explanations, for convenience labelling them 'Learning' and 'Two-part Desert'.

i) *Learning.* The basic idea here is that although most subjects began Stage 1 with a clear understanding of how to maximise joint payoffs, perhaps many of them had not worked out in advance the traditional game theoretic solution of splitting the gains approximately equally (C_3). It is often implicitly, and sometimes explicitly, assumed that even if individuals do not initially and intuitively conform with conventional notions of rationality, they would choose to do so if the issues were explained to them and/or they tend to do so after gaining experience and feedback from bargaining or market environments (see, for example, Smith (1989) and Harrison (1989)).

In Stage 1 of our experiment, most subjects had the experience of bargaining with a succession of between five and nine other subjects. If the general experience of bargaining – and in particular, the experience by 'irrational' subjects of coming into bargaining contact with 'rational' players – lies behind the contrast between Stage 1 and Stage 2 behaviour, we might expect to see signs of it in the course of Stage 1. In other words, we might expect to observe a general shift in favour of C_3, equal splitting of the gains from trade, as Stage 1 progressed.

To examine this possibility, we took each round in turn and pooled the data from across all twelve groups from pairs which began with unequal endow-

[5] This is somewhat reminiscent of the shift observed in Hoffman and Spitzer's (1985) experiment between 'coinflip with no moral authority' and 'hash game with moral authority'.

Table 5. Regressing gaindiff on startdiff

Stage 1

Round	No. of Bargains	Coefficient	*t* statistic
1	36	−0.579	− 5.28
2	38	−0.675	−. 7.91
3	39	−0.634	− 8.31
4	40	−0.673	− 6.41
5	37	−0.794	−10.85
6	34	−0.494	− 4.94
7	35	−0.544	− 6.03
8	29	−0.889	−16.08
9	20	−0.503	− 4.24

Stage 2

Round	No. of Bargains	Coefficient	*t* statistic
1	22	+0.121	+0.98
2	22	+0.011	+0.08
3	21	−0.181	−1.28
4	20	−0.210	−3.83
5	20	−0.259	−2.81
6	18	−0.257	−3.33
7	18	−0.162	−1.08
8	12	−0.015	−0.32
9	13	+0.041	+0.64

(Note: Only cases where initial endowments differed are included)

ments. Within each round, the different pairs are independent of each other. For each pair we calculated the values of two variables: Startdiff – the difference between the two subjects' initial endowments; and Gaindiff – the difference between their respective gains from trade. For those who split the gains from trade equally, Gaindiff would take a value of zero, whereas for those who split the total payoffs equally, Gaindiff would have the same absolute value as Startdiff but the opposite sign. For each round in turn, we regressed Gaindiff on Startdiff, suppressing the constant. If there were a significant learning effect in the direction of the Nash solution, we should expect to observe the estimated coefficient tending towards zero as subjects gained experience from successive rounds of bargaining. However, as Table 5 shows, there is no evidence of any such tendency.

There remains the possibility that learning took place *between* Stages 1 and 2, i.e. when subjects were reflecting on their experiences after Stage 1 and/or when considering the details of the two follow-up experiments, one of which was Stage 2. We cannot rule out this possibility – although it would not account for the Hoffman-Spitzer results, where those randomised to the 'game trigger – moral authority' combination had no more opportunity to learn than any of the other subsamples exposed to different combinations of stimuli. Still, even though we have no evidence to support the learning explanation, neither do we have sufficient evidence to decisively reject it. However, a second possibility perhaps provides a more convincing explanation.

ii) *Two-part Desert.* If we go back to Hoffman and Spitzer's (1985 pp.264–5) discussion of desert, we note the emphasis placed upon the idea that desert derives from the "expenditure of effort", and the reference to the equity principle "that people allocate payments so as to equalise individual ratios between payments and intrinsic inputs". Up to this point we have supposed this to mean that in Stage 1, where initial endowments are allocated at random and are acquired effortlessly, there is no desert basis for any unequal division of the total payoff; whereas in Stage 2, we have assumed that the wordscores are an acceptable index of effort, and that the ratio of wordscores provides the measure of the ratio of intrinsic inputs which the division of total payoffs would seek to reflect.

However, the wordscores and the endowments they generate are not the only inputs into the bargaining process. On their own the initial endowments do not generate any gains from trade. To achieve such gains requires some purposeful expenditure of effort to work out how to maximise joint payoffs, and some further effort to arrive at an agreement about the division of the total, and then to complete the task of actually drawing up the contract, updating Record Sheets, etc. There are therefore two parts to the input of effort: the initial effort with the wordscore task, and the subsequent effort involved in achieving the potential gains from trade. In the wordscore exercise, each subject tackles the same task under the same conditions; but each works quite independently so that it is straightforward and salient to associate differential earnings with different inputs of effort, and to regard such differentials as deserved.

In the *quite distinct* bargaining exercise, both subjects in any pair collaborate to perform the set of tasks that generate the gains from trade. They are now mixing their labour not simply with nature, but with each other's. Given the difficulty of disentangling their respective contributions, it may seem fair to them to share equally the resulting gains from trade. This would correspond to Güth's 'personal investment standard', a presumption of equal input when effort is difficult to quantify (Güth 1988, p.707).

Thus in Stage 2, where there are two distinct phases of activity, both generating some deserved part of the final payoffs, C_3 behaviour is consistent with two-part desert. On the other hand in Stage 1, where the first phase of activity consists of an allocation of endowments which involves no effort differential, two-part desert suggests an equal division of the final joint total, i.e. C_2 behaviour. If a substantial proportion of our sample acted according to *this* interpretation of the concept of desert, it not only accounts for the marked shift from C_2 to C_3 between Stages 1 and 2, but also for the relative unimportance of C_5 even in Stage 2.

However, we note that even if this interpretation is correct, the results in Table 4 suggest that there were also significant proportions of the sample who operated on a different basis, some as egalitarians and some as utilitarians. Thus in Stage 1, initial differentials were maintained, or even extended (ie. $C_3 + C_5$) in 27.2% of cases – indicating, perhaps, the coming together of pairs of subjects who both subscribed to a Nash solution and/or at least one member of the pair pursuing his self interest as effectively as a typical utilitarian. Alongside that, we see that in Stage 2, 34.3% of cases ($C_2 + C_4$) involved agreements which divided the gains from exchange so that they partially or completely offset the initial wordscore differential, which might suggest that at least one member of the pair was arguing with some success for either a moderate, or more often a strict, egalitarian solution.

We also raise the possibility that when the different types come together in different proportions, different 'group ethics' may arise. For example, Table 4 shows that Groups 1.4, 1.6 and 1.8 exhibit rather similar patterns of behaviour, although they are very different from the patterns exhibited by Groups 1.5 and 1.7 which are also quite similar to one another.

It would be interesting, and in line with some recent critiques of conventional game theoretic analysis, such as those by Binmore (1987, 1988) and Sugden (1986), to consider the implications of a model in which the population, consisting of the three main 'types' discussed in this paper, comes together in a series of pairwise bargaining situations of the kind produced by our experiment. Depending on the relative values attached by people of the different types to their 'pure' self-interest and to the notion of fairness which they favour, the set of strategies and solutions might be quite rich. Such a model is beyond the scope of the present paper, but we consider that the evidence reported in Table 4 indicates the need for models of this kind which do not assume homogeneous players. The relative stability of the within-Stage coefficients in Table 5 may indicate that, rather than one type tending to dominate or drive out the others after repeated interaction, the different types may co-exist and produce reasonably stable aggregate behaviour.

5 Conclusion

The two-part version of desert theory, which our evidence tentatively supports, is consistent with the proposition that many people believe that when different individuals have *a similar ability and opportunity* to put in effort, those that put in more effort should get a greater reward because they are relatively deserving. In the experiment where the participants' initial endowments correspond to their level of effort this belief was reflected in the subsequent protection of the initial endowment differentials and the equal sharing of the fruits of a collaborative effort in bargaining. By contrast, when initial endowments were determined by chance, the majority of participants did not attempt to sustain the differentials in the bargaining that followed.

Our results are consistent with earlier indications that bargaining behaviour is sensitive to non-monetary motivations. Moreover, our findings endorse Thaler's (1988, p.205) view that people cannot simply be divided into 'fairmen' who divide everything equally and 'gamesmen' who always act as selfish utility maximisers, but rather that many individuals prefer more money to less but also place a value on fairness and are able to strike a reasonably sophisticated balance between the two. To the extent that notions of fairness affect people's attitudes and behaviour regarding the maintenance or adjustment of differentials, and the distribution of income and wealth, they are clearly liable to play a role in important policy decisions, so that in modelling behaviour we would do well to incorporate attitudes to fairness at the outset.

References

Binmore K (1987) Modeling rational players: Part I. Economics and Philosophy 3:179–214

Binmore K (1988) Modeling rational players: Part II, Economics and Philosophy 4:9–55

Güth W (1988) On the behavioural approach to distributive justice – A theoretical and empirical investigation. In: Applied Behavioural Economics Vol II Maital S (ed) Wheatsheaf Brighton

Harrison GW (1989) Rational expectations and experimental methods. In: Rational Expectations and Efficiency in Futures Markets Goss B (ed) Routledge London

Hoffman E, Spitzer ML (1982) The Coase theorem: Some experimental tests. Journal of Law and Economics 25:73–98

Hoffman E, Spitzer ML (1985) Entitlements, rights and fairness: An experimental examination of subjects' concepts of distributive justice. Journal of Legal Studies 14:259–297

Kahneman D, Knetsch JL, Thaler R (1986) Fairness as a constraint on profit seeking: Entitlements in the market. American Economic Review 76:728–741

Ochs J, Roth A (1989) An experimental study of sequential bargaining. American Economic Review 79:355–384

Rawls J (1971) A theory of justice. Oxford University Press

Sher G (1987) Desert. Princeton University Press

Smith VL (1989) Theory, experiments and economics. Journal of Economic Perspectives 3:151–169

Sugden R (1986) The economics of rights, co-operation and welfare. Blackwell Oxford

Thaler RH (1988) The ultimatum game. Journal of Economic Perspectives 2:195–206

Veljanovski CG (1981) Wealth maximisation, law and ethics – on the limits of economic efficiency. International Review of Law and Economics 1:5–28

Expected Utility Theory and the Experimentalists

Glenn W. Harrison[1]

Department of Economics, College of Business Administration, University of South Carolina, Columbia, SC29208, USA

Abstract: The experimental evidence against expected utility theory is, on balance, either uninformative or unconvincing. When one modifies the experiments to mitigate these criticisms the evidence tends to support traditional theory.

JEL-Classification System-Numbers: D81, C91, B41

Expected Utility Theory has been under severe attack in recent years. The source of this attack has been the observation of apparently robust behavioral anomalies in decisions that individual experimental subjects make in controlled environments. The popular implication of these observations is that Expected Utility Theory (EUT) is systematically misleading as a descriptive model of human behavior under uncertainty. Many alternative models of individual choice behavior have been proposed that can account for some or all of the alleged anomalies. We argue that the experiments in question do not meet widely accepted sufficient conditions for a valid controlled experiment proposed by Smith [1982; pp. 930 ff.]. Moreover, when some of those experiments are modified to satisfy those conditions the anomalies in question either vanish or significantly diminish.

Four conditions are proposed by Smith [1982]. The first is *Nonsatiation* in the reward medium v: utility $U(v)$ is a monotone increasing function of v. Thus we can expect that a choice that generates v' will be preferred to a choice that generates v'' whenever $v' > v''$.

The second condition is *Saliency* of the reward medium: there is a mapping, perhaps only implicit in the rules of the experiment, between rewards and the messages m of the institution under study. Thus we can expect that a message (e.g., a bid, or a stated preference) m' that maps into v' will be observed, instead of a message m'' that maps into v'', whenever $v' > v''$.

The third conditions is *Dominance* of the rewards over the subjective costs (or benefits) to a subject from participating in the experimental task. In practice this

---

[1] Dewey H. Johnson Professor of Economics, Department of Economics, College of Business Administration, University of South Carolina. I am grateful for comments from seminar participants at the University of Melbourne, University of South Carolina, University of Stockholm, and the University of Western Ontario. John Hey provided a firm, but sympathetic, editorial hand.

condition requires that the rewards corresponding to the null hypothesis are "perceptibly and motivationally greater" than the rewards corresponding to the alternative hypothesis. Assume for the moment that each hypothesis refers to a specific message: m_o for the null and m_a for the alternative. In this case we require that the rewards associated with these two messages, v_o and v_a respectively, be such that $v_0 > v_a + \delta$, where δ is the subjective cost to the agent from sending m_o rather than m_a.[2]

Figure 1 illustrates these concepts for two experimental designs, *A* and *B*. The payoff function for each experiment is drawn so that they each have the same payoff v_o for the same message m_o. However, they differ greatly with respect to the payoff under the alternative hypothesis, message m_a. For the value of δ shown Experiment *A* fails to satisfy the Dominance precept whereas experiment *B* does satisfy it. The implication is that one should avoid an experimental design such as *A* in favor of one such as *B* whenever possible.

Experimentalists do not have any objective notion of the value of δ for a wide range of tasks, and it is unlikely that any "objective" measures of δ for a given subject pool in a given task environment are likely to gain wide acceptance. Nonetheless, it is always possible to report the *design* of a given experiment *conditional on a range of values for* δ that can be widely accepted as plausible. Assume that $\hat{\delta}$ is "the" value of δ that is accepted ($\hat{\delta} > 0$). Then any experimental design such that $v_0 \leq v_a + \hat{\delta}$ will be said to fail the Dominance requirement conditional on $\hat{\delta}$ as the assumed perceptive and motivational threshold. Much like Good Bayesians[3] report posterior-based inferences for a wide class of

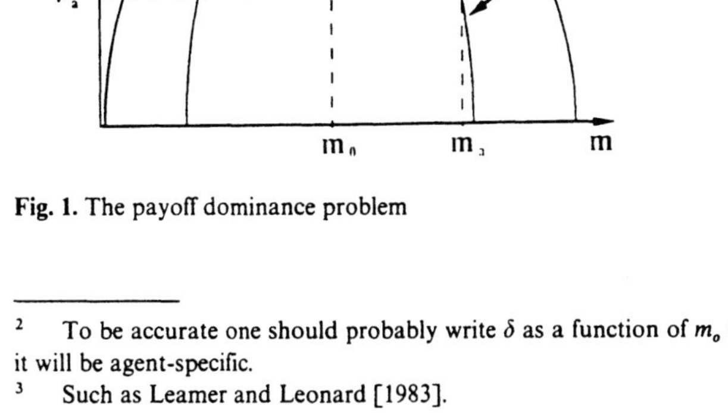

Fig. 1. The payoff dominance problem

[2] To be accurate one should probably write δ as a function of m_o and m_a, as well as noting that it will be agent-specific.

[3] Such as Leamer and Leonard [1983].

priors, so should Good Experimentalists report the range of values for δ such that their experimental design ensures that $v_0 > v_a + \delta$ for given v_o and v_a. In such cases the reader of the study can draw his own inferences from the data as a function of his own priors over $\hat{\delta}$.

An important practical extension of the concept of Dominance is required when one or more of the hypotheses is not simple. Assume that we have a simple point-null hypothesis (e.g., $m = m_o$) and a composite alternative hypothesis (e.g., $m \neq m_o$). In this case there typically exists, for a given δ, a set of messages $\bar{m}$ arbitrarily close to m_o, such that $v(\bar{m}) \geq v_0(m_0) - \delta$. Conversely, there exists a set of messages $\hat{m}$ such that $v(\hat{m}) < v_0(m_0) - \delta$. We may then say that no observations in the set $\bar{m}$ can be claimed to satisfy the Dominance requirement; one can only make such claims about observations in the set $\hat{m}$. Figure 2 illustrates these concepts. Harrison [1989] [1992] demonstrates that many experiments have been inadvertently designed such that virtually all of the observations fall in the set $\bar{m}$, conditional on plausibly small values of δ. Thus one must nihilistically insist that the subjects have a sufficiently low threshold δ, perhaps even claiming $\delta = 0$, in order to maintain the conclusion that such observations allow one to reject the null hypothesis.[4]

We argue that many of the experimental anomalies that are claimed to violate EUT do not satisfy the Saliency requirement or, if they do, generally fail to satisfy the Dominance requirement for plausible (perceptual or motivational) threshold values. The anomalies examined here that *do* survive the Dominance requirement turn out to be the clear exception rather than the "rule". On

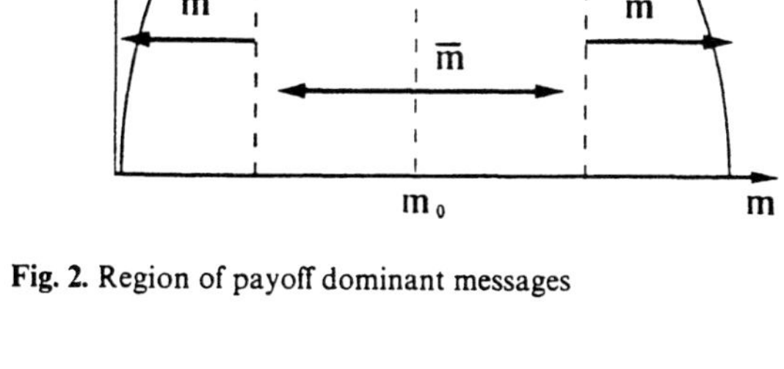

Fig. 2. Region of payoff dominant messages

[4] If δ is strictly positive then there *always* exists *some* sub-optimal message that fails the Dominance requirement. In practice, however, the discrete nature of individual behavioral responses will often provide a natural solution to this nihilist's dilemma.

balance, then, the experimental evidence against EUT evaluated here is either uninformative or unconvincing.

It is appropriate to focus on four groups of experiments that have played what I would argue are an infamous historical role in the critique of EUT and the received theory of choice under uncertainty.[5] The first is the Allais Paradox experiment devised by Allais [1953]. The second set is the Preference Reversal experiment developed by Grether and Plott [1979]. The third set is a group of simple choice experiments underlying the heuristics that are rationalized by the Prospect Theory of Kahneman and Tversky [1979]. The final set is the test of Bayes Rule devised by Grether [1981]; although not formally a component of EUT, Bayes Rule lies at the core of most interesting economic models of behavior under uncertainty.

1 The Allais Paradox

1.1 The Experiment

Consider the "probability triangle" in Figure 3 defined over the probabilities of three monetary prizes: a low prize P_L, an intermediate prize P_I, and a high prize P_H, with $P_L < P_I < P_H$. Let π_L, π_I and π_H be the probabilities that each of P_L, P_I and P_H will eventuate in a given lottery. Because $\pi_L + \pi_I + \pi_H = 1$, we can express π_I implicitly in terms of π_L and π_H (i.e., given values of π_L and π_H, π_I is uniquely determined).

The Allais Paradox, or AP, can be conveniently represented in a probability triangle.[6] Consider four separate lotteries shown in Figure 3 as A, A^*, B and B^*. Note that A is related to A^* in the same way as B is related to B^*: just increase π_H by a certain amount (e.g., 0.10) and increase π_L by a certain amount (e.g., 0.01), thereby implicitly decreasing π_I by a certain amount (e.g., 0.11). From the perspective of EUT the crucial feature of this configuration is that the chords AA^* and BB^* are parallel straight lines.

---

[5] Many other experiments have tested aspects of EUT, but none have been quite as influential as the three considered here. Harrison [1989] [1992] and Drago and Heywood [1989] consider a wide range of experiments and argue that they suffer from the payoff Dominance problem in one way or another. In many cases a cursory reading of the experimental procedures of an experiment are enough for one to decide that the decisions could not possibly satisfy the Dominance criteria. For example, Camerer [1989] uses a random-selection rule in which 1-in-N subjects are actually paid. As N becomes large a lack of Dominance is assured. (Starmer and Sugden [1990] study the effectiveness of this random-selection procedure, with mixed results: see Davis and Holt [1993; p. 452–455] for further discussion).

[6] Davis and Holt [1993; p. 438–442] provide a nice exposition of this pedagogic device.

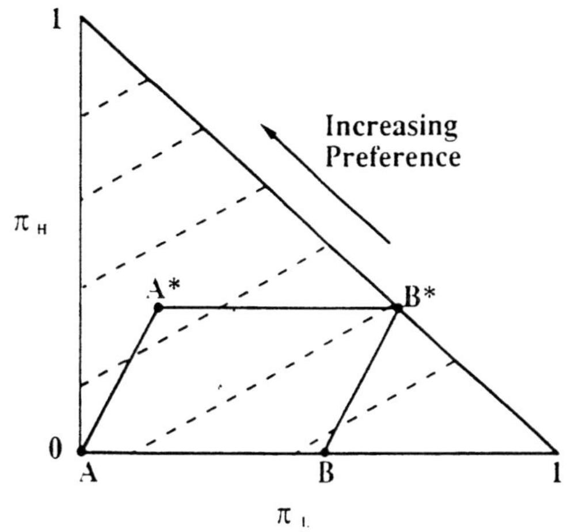

Fig. 3. The Allais paradox

EUT assumes that the expected utility of any bundle of uncertain prizes is equal to the utility of each prize weighted simply by the probability of that prize. Thus the indifference curves of a non-satiated agent are straight lines, as shown by dashed lines in Figure 3. The agent whose tastes are depicted in Figure 3 would choose A^* over A and B^* over B when asked to make these two bilateral choices.

An important property of the slopes of the indifference curves of an agent obeying EUT is that they depend on his attitudes to risk (e.g., see Machina [1986; p. 126–7]). A risk-neutral agent will have indifference curves with slope $\tau = (P_I - P_L)/(P_H - P_I)$. A risk-preferring agent will have indifference curves that are relatively flatter than τ. Crucially, a risk-averse (RA) agent will have indifference curves that are steeper than τ. Figure 4 illustrates why this is important: for any AP configuration of lotteries, there exists an attitude to risk such that the agent is indifferent between the lotteries he is asked to choose between.[7] Typically the experiments testing the AP do not allow subjects to report indifference.[8]

With this background, what is the AP? The AP refers to two observed patterns of choice: (1) subjects who choose A over A^* but choose B^* over B, and (2) subjects who choose A^* over A but choose B over B^*. Conlisk [1989] found (in

[7] In Figure 4 we draw the case of a RA agent and the normal AP configuration with the chord AA^* steeper than τ (for simplicity we assume here that $\tau = 1$, although this is not the case for the prizes considered later). Clearly our claim is general. If the chord were flatter than τ, we need only depict a sufficiently risk-loving agent's preferences. It is similarly obvious that a RA agent could well have indifference curves even steeper than the slope of the AA^* chord.

[8] Exceptions include Battalio, Kagel and Jiranyakul [1990] (who observed few subjects reporting indifference) and Hey and DiCagno [1990].

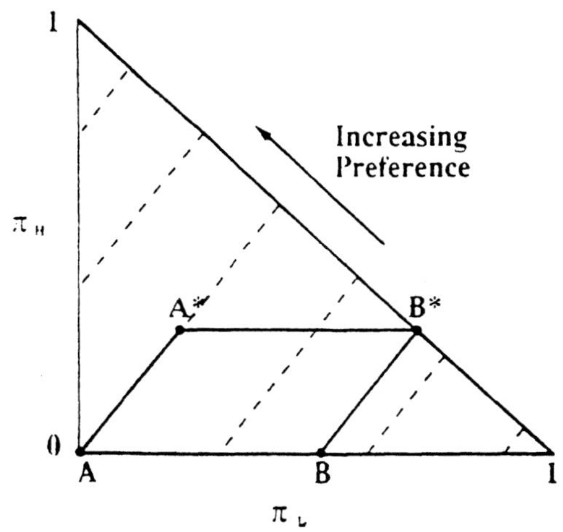

Fig. 4. The Allais paradox with particular risk-neutral preferences

his "Basic Version") that 50.4% of 236 University of California at San Diego economics undergraduates chose either (1) or (2) when their payoffs were hypothetical and the prizes expressed in terms of "millions of dollars". Moreover, the vast majority (86.5%) of those 119 students chose pattern (1), implying that there is a systematic pattern of responses.

In what sense should we call the observed behavior "paradoxical"? For the agent depicted in Figure 3, either of pattern (1) or (2) violates EUT. In general, violations occur true for any agent whose indifference curves do not overlap the chord AA^* (and hence also do not overlap BB^*). What about the agent depicted in Figure 4? Forced by experimental design to make a choice between A and A^*, he would no doubt "flip a coin". Similarly for his forced choice between B and B^*. The result, with a large enough sample of such agents, would match exactly the 50.4% rate of AP behavior observed by Conlisk [1988]. In this, deliberately extreme, case the AP behavior is purely an artifact of the experimenter requiring the subject to report a strict preference. The subject foregoes zero expected income or utility

Convenient as this argument may be for EUT, it is clearly too strong. First, it requires that the agent in question have attitudes to risk that imply indifference curves that precisely match the chord AA^*. Although the degree of risk aversion that might be required in Figure 4 is not implausible, the requirement that it be a specific degree of risk aversion is implausible. Second, we require that all agents in the sample have the same attitude to risk. This further stretches the plausibility of our argument, since AP behavior has been observed in hypothetical questionnaires using a wide range of subjects who plausibly have a wide range of attitudes to risk.

What our argument does identify, especially in the polar form of Figure 4, are two potentially important treatments in the design of AP experiments. One is to allow subjects to report indifference, given that "as if" AP anomalies could be observed under the null hypothesis of EUT if one does not permit such reports. The other treatment is to control for the risk attitudes of agents, so that we can ensure (under the null hypothesis) that we have a design such as in Figure 3 instead of a design such as in Figure 4.

To control for risk attitudes we adopt the lottery procedure of Roth and Malouf [1979] and Berg, Daley, Dickhaut and O'Brien [1986]. This procedure allows the experimenter to induce "as if" risk-neutral behavior by conducting an experiment in which the rewards are units of probability that a subject will win some monetary prize. A convenient way to operationalize this is to reward subjects with "lottery tickets", with every extra ticket earned increasing the probability that the monetary prize will be won. Irrespective of the subject's attitudes to risk defined over monetary prizes, this procedure induces risk neutrality with respect to the reward medium of the experiment (lottery tickets). Thus we redefine P_L, P_I and P_H in terms of numbers of lottery tickets, and denote the monetary lottery prize M; the subject receives zero cash payoff if he loses the lottery, and $M > 0$ if he wins the lottery.

There has been some debate over the ability of this procedure to induce risk-neutral behavior in certain experimental contexts (e.g., the first-price sealed-bid auctions of Cox, Smith and Walker [1985]). However, Berg, Daley, Dickhaut and O'Brien [1986] have tested the procedure in a binary choice context such as employed here, an they found that the procedure indeed induced the predicted choices.[9] Moreover, it can be shown that this particular test of the lottery procedure does *not* fail the Dominance requirement (see Harrison [1992; p.1430, fn.5]). This point is especially important in terms of our present design objectives: to construct a Salient and Dominant test of the AP.

1.2 Saliency: The Conlisk Experiments

Despite the voluminous literature on the AP, Conlisk [1989] appears to have been the first to adopt salient rewards. He gave 53 subjects, drawn from the same population as his non-salient experiments discussed above, the standard binary choices over the following prospects: A: certainty of \$5; A^*: 1/100 chance of \$0, 89/100 chance of \$5, and 10/100 chance of \$25; B: 89/100 chance of \$0, and 11/100 chance of \$5; and B^*: 90/100 chance of \$0, and 10/100 chance of \$25. He found that only 3 of his subjects, or 5.7% of his sample, chose prospects that violate EUT. His results are presented in Table 1.

---

[9] As a slight qualification, note that their test compared the choices of "as if" risk-averse agents with "as if" risk-preferring agents. They did not study the behavior of "as if" risk-neutral agents. However, their test does demonstrate that there is nothing in the binary choice context that might invalidate the lottery procedure, which is the issue in debate.

Table 1. Results from selected allais paradox experiments

Experiment	Payoffs	Number of Subjects	Percentage of Outcomes				
			EUT-consistent		EUT violations		
			AB	*A*B**	*A*B*	*AB**	Total
AP0	Hypothetical	20	0	65	0	35	100%
Conlisk	Hypothetical	236	8	7	42	44	100%
AP1	Salient	20	0	85	0	15	100%
Conlisk	Salient	53	0	94	0	6	100%
AP2	Salient & Dominant	20	0	95	0	5	100%

Reassuring as these results might seem for EUT, two doubts remain. First, Conlisk [1989; p. 34] also observed that the AP anomalies disappeared almost completely in a practice round using the same subjects but with hypothetical payoffs. Thus it is not at all obvious that Saliency, as distinct perhaps from the absence of dizziness due to payoffs not having the word *million* attached, is the savior of EUT.

The second doubt concerns the splitting of the sample: about half of the subjects chose between *A* and *A**, while the other half chose between *B* and *B**. The reported results refer to the pooling of the choices of these sub-samples as if they had all been reported by the full sample. Sample size is not the issue here, since the results are so overwhelmingly consistent with one or other hypothesis (happily, EUT). Rather the problem is that one must implicitly assume that the tastes of the two sub-samples are "sufficiently homogeneous" that how one sub-sample behaves on the *AA** choice can be validly compared to how the other sub-sample behaves on the *BB** choice. Requiring an auxiliary assumption such as this biases the design against EUT. The evidence strongly supports EUT, of course, so this is not a decisive problem with the design.

1.3 Saliency and Dominance

Without controlling for the risk attitudes of subjects, and ensuring Dominance, it is not possible to claim that observed AP anomalies are due to a failure of EUT. AP anomalies appear to disappear completely when one merely makes the rewards Salient, as just noted, but it is not obvious that Saliency is the key treatment. Therefore we designed and implemented a new experiment to focus on these issues.[10]

[10] The sample sizes for many of the new experiments reported here are quite small, so the *precise* quantitative results deserve to be interpreted with a grain of salt.

Each subject was asked to make two binary choices. The prospects employed were: *A*: 500 cents with certainty; *A**: 1/100 chance of 0 cents, 89/100 chance of 500 cents, and 10/100 chance of 2000 cents; *B*: 89/100 chance of 0 cents, and 11/100 chance of 500 cents; and *B**: 90/100 chance of 0 cents, and 10/100 chance of 2000 cents. Three experimental conditions were employed. In condition *AP0* all payoffs were hypothetical. In condition *AP1* all payoffs were as stated above. A risk-neutral subject could expect to earn $8.50 in each of these two conditions if he made the choices predicted by EUT.

In condition *AP2* all payoffs were as stated above except that the word "cents" was replaced with "points" and it was explained that every point earned would equal one extra "lottery ticket". Each extra lottery ticket gave the subject an extra 1% probability of winning C$40 in the final lottery. The value $40 was chosen because that implies the same expected value of the experiment to a risk-neutral agent in condition *AP2* as in *AP1*: we wanted to ensure that expected rewards were comparable under the null hypotheses in condition *AP2* (viz., risk-neutral EUT-consistent choices) and condition *AP1* (viz., EUT-consistent choices).[11] Note also that the risk-neutral subject in condition *AP2* foregoes $1.45 in *each* binary choice if he does not obey EUT. The same values apply in condition *AP1* if one makes the auxiliary assumption that the subject is risk-neutral. The entire session lasted about 15 minutes in each condition.[12] Thus we would argue that the incentives that subjects faced satisfied the Dominance requirement.

The results of our experiments are reported in Table 1. We find that all of the observed choices that violate EUT are of one kind: *AB**, in which the prospect with no uncertainty (prospect *A*) seduces subjects to violate EUT. When payoffs are not Salient EUT is violated by 35% of the subjects. When payoffs are Salient, however, the percentage of subjects violating EUT drops to 15% (condition *AP1*) and 5% (condition *AP2*). We therefore observe a very powerful effect simply from ensuring Salient payoffs.

The strength of the effect of Salience makes it difficult to observe any strong effect from adding Dominance: although the drop in EUT violations from 15% to 5% is in the predicted direction, the sample size does not allow us to claim that this is a statistically significant decline.[13]

---

[11] A subject behaving in accord with EUT could expect to earn 850 tickets in condition *AP2*. The maximum number of lottery tickets that could be earned by certain choices and some good luck is 4000. Thus the subject would have an expected probability of $850 \div 4000 = 0.2125$ of winning the monetary prize *M*. For the expected payoff to be $8.50 we therefore set $M = \$8.50 \div 0.2125 = \$40$.

[12] These sessions were conducted after the subjects had participated in first-price sealed-bid auction experiments such as those reported in Harrison [1989]. In each case the previous experiment had employed exactly the same payment condition. Thus the subjects in condition *AP2* were already familiar with the lottery procedure (although it was explained to them afresh). All subjects were drawn from the undergraduate economics student population at the University of Western Ontario.

[13] To see this point, consider a simple χ^2 test of the null hypothesis that the observed choice frequency under *AP2* is the same as the expected choice frequency found in *AP1* (i.e., that we only expect to see an effect from Saliency). We then have $\chi^2 = 1.568$ with 3 degrees of freedom, and are unable to reject the null hypothesis at any standard significance level.

2 Preference Reversals

2.1 The Experiment

Grether and Plott [1979], hereafter GP, design a beautiful experiment to test a phenomenon discovered by psychologists known as "preference reversals". These reversals involve the same subject stating that he prefers one wager to another, and separately reporting "selling prices" for those wagers that imply a different preference. It is as if his preference over the two wagers reverses as we move from one preference-elicitation procedure to another. What is so nice about the GP experiment is that it was designed with economists in mind, and addresses many of the sneaking suspicions that economists have about such results from experimental psychology. What is so disturbing about the GP experiment is that, notwithstanding these design features, preference reversals persist.

The basic experiment of GP (their Experiment 1) consists of three Parts. In Part 1 the subject is asked to state a preference for one wager over another (indifference was allowed). Three pairs of wagers are evaluated in this manner. In Part 3 the subject is likewise asked to state his preference for one of the two wagers in another three pairs. Thus in Parts 1 and 3 we have stated preferences for six distinct pairs of wagers. In Part 2 the subject is asked to state selling prices for each of the 12 wagers involved in Parts 1 and 3. The Becker, DeGroot and Marschak [1964] (BDM) procedure is employed to elicit these selling prices, with buying prices drawn at random from a uniform distribution defined over the interval 0 to 999. This procedure is designed to elicit the certainty-equivalent of an arbitrary risky prospect.[14]

Two methods of financial reward were employed by GP. In the first method 44 subjects received $7 for simply completing the experiment, irrespective of their decisions. In the second method 46 subjects were given a $7 credit and then told that at the end of the experiment one of their 18 decisions (6 reported preferences and 12 valuations) would be selected and used to determine if they earn more or less money.[15] It was possible for the subjects to lose up to $2 if

[14] The task is to devise a procedure that gives subjects a financial incentive to truthfully state their certainty-equivalent for a given wager. BDM solve this problem by asking the subject to state a minimum "selling price" for the wager and then randomly choosing a "buying price" for the wager. If the buying price exceeds the stated selling price the subject receives the former price; if not, he gets to play the wager. Providing that this buying price is randomly determined and is independent of the stated selling price at any stage, it can be easily shown that the subject maximizes the expected utility of the reward by setting his selling price equal to this monetary equivalent of the basic wager. Harrison [1992; pp. 1428–9] explains how one evaluates the strength of the financial incentives under this procedure.

[15] Holt [1986a] has shown that this procedure, of selecting one decision to reward subjects, may induce "as if" preference reversal behavior when the Independence Axiom of standard expected

they had some bad luck, leaving them assured of a net take home payoff of at least $5. We will focus here on subjects that were financially motivated to make better decisions.

There were two early attempts to modify the GP design to determine if the reversal phenomenon is robust. The first is by Pommerehne, Schneider and Zweifel [1982]. They argue that the subjects in the GP experiment faced very little incentive to make correct decisions. However, it is not at all clear that they have in mind anything with the word "incentives" that is, or should be, of interest to economists. In order to "create a more stimulating situation" (p. 569) for the subjects they increased the face value of the prizes in the wagers. They did this by denominating the prizes in Swiss Francs, so that a prize of US$3.86 in the GP experiment would now be shown as Fr.386. Clearly increasing the *face value* alone will not help matters: if the exchange rate between Swiss Francs and dollars were 0.01, the prizes would be identical in terms of purchasing power (give or take epsilon due to violations of PPP).[16] Simply denominating the currency units more finely cannot possibly help matters. If it does induce more careful decision making then the subject must be suffering from some "numeraire illusion" which is not good for experimental design or control.[17]

In any case, the subjects did not even receive the stated face value after all. In fact the experiments used "play money", with subject earnings converted into real money at the end of the experiment at a conversion rate that was unknown to them at the time of their decisions. This rate was determined, ex post the subjects' decisions, so as to divide up a fixed total of Fr.2000 between 84 subjects. This implies that each subject would have received around US$13.6 over 12 decisions on average, or US$1.09 per decision on average. We therefore agree with Grether and Plott [1982; p. 575] that "it is not obvious that the incentives were greater" than in the original GP experiments.

The second attempt to modify the design of the GP experiments is by Reilly [1982]. He ran two series of experiments. The first series, his Stage 1, is virtually

---

utility theory is violated. This is a comforting result, since that is arguably the one axiom of expected utility theory that is the least damaging to dispose of (see Machina [1982]). It should be noted that GP use this procedure, following BDM, to avoid "wealth effects" from early earnings or losses from contaminating responses in later decisions. Given that truthful revelation is a strongly dominant strategy in the BDM elicitation procedure, it is not clear why "wealth effects' should matter at all.

[16] As it turns out, the exchange rate was about Fr.1.82 over 1980–81, so the face value of Fr.386 would have been about US $212.

[17] Unfortunately this procedure of increasing the face value of experimental rewards in order to "improve subject motivation" or to "improve statistical inference" is all too common. Many experimentalists denominate their payoffs in "francs" or "pesos" rather than "dollars or cents", without any clear notion as to why this should encourage better decisions: e.g., see Forsythe, Palfrey and Plott [1982; p. 542]. The fact that this design feature has not (yet) been associated with odd experimental results does not justify regarding it as a "successful" design innovation (Plott and Sunder [1982, p. 667]). This argument has nothing to do with the possible benefits of conducting experiments in some currency other than cash: see Roth and Malouf [1979] and Berg, Daley, Dickhaut and O'Brien [1986].

a replication of GP[18] but with slightly different prizes in the basic wagers. He replicated their main results.

Contemplation of subject behavior during Stage 1 led Reilly [1982] to adopt a number of design features in Stage 2 that were "... intended to strengthen monetary incentives and reduce confusion among the subjects" (p. 580). These new design features were: (i) the use of smaller groups of subjects in any one session, to encourage the asking of clarifying questions; (ii) an increase in the running time of the experiment, so as not to press any subjects into unduly hasty decisions; (iii) clarification that the rewards were not hypothetical; (iv) the provision of the expected value of the wager to each subject; and (v) the use of the interval (−400,1400) rather than (0,999) in order to generate buyout prices in the BDM procedure. These changes in design were associated with modest but significant reductions in the extent of observed preference reversals. Nonetheless, the phenomenon persists.

2.2 *Inferences from the Experiment*

As we have noted above, the preference reversal phenomenon discovered in financially motivated subjects by GP has been replicated and found to be robust. One implication is that we should embrace tractable modifications of standard expected utility theory that allow "as if" preference reversals (see Holt [1986a], Karni and Safra [1987], Loomes and Sugden [1983], Machina [1982] [1987] and Segal [1988] for careful arguments along these lines, and Cox and Epstein [1989] for experiment that are inconsistent with one of these modifications). Another implication, far less attractive to economists, is that we must pay theoretical and empirical attention to the way in which valuations or preferences are assumed to be elicited or communicated in decision-making environments.

[18] Actually there is one disparity between the procedures that Reilly [1982] used and those of GP. In conversation Reilly has pointed out that he randomized over the six lottery pairs when deciding on the payoff to subjects. If a given lottery pair was selected for payoff, the subjects direct preferences would be used to determine which lottery of that pair would be played out using the BDM procedure and the subjects reported valuation for that lottery. In conversation Grether confirms that GP actually randomized over the eighteen decisions. In each experiment the subjects were told only that one decision would be used to determine the payoff. We shall assume that subjects interpreted this as implying what was actually done in the GP experiment. Subjects in our replication of GP were explicitly told at the outset that one of their 18 decisions would be selected.

2.3 *The Cost of Misbehavior*

One question that is typically not addressed in the three experimental studies reviewed above is *how* inconsistent are the reported decisions of subjects? Vague statements by Pommerehne, Schneider and Zweifel [1982; p. 569–570] about subjects not being motivated, or sensing small differences in payoffs, can readily be made explicit.

The opportunity cost of an inconsistent report is the expected income that is foregone by not reporting consistently. There are many ways to make consistent reports, and we make the simplest possible assumptions. Specifically, assume that the subject reports his ordinal preferences in Parts 1 and 3 according to his true (consistent) preferences. Then the entire "cost" of any misbehavior is borne in the Part 2 decisions, the selling price reports. Without any difference to the results reported below, assume that the valuations elicited for one type of wager (the "P-bet", in the parlance used in this literature) is in accord with the subject's true preferences. Thus the "false report" that may imply a preference reversal is the valuation elicited for the other wager (the paired "$-bet"). We evaluate the foregone expected income of this false report. If the ordinal ranking implied by the reported valuations is the same as the directly-elicited ordinal ranking of Parts 1 and 3, then no preference reversal is implied and the foregone expected income is of course zero.

It should also be remembered that any single decision by the subjects in these experiments had only a 1-in-18 chance of being used by the experimenter to decide the final payoff. Thus the cost of an inconsistent decision at any stage is to be divided by 18 to obtain the appropriate cost on a "per decision" basis. We use these procedures to evaluate the opportunity cost of inconsistency in the experiments conducted by Reilly [1982] and a replication of the GP experiment.[19]

A *The Reilly Experiments*

In his Stage 2 sessions Reilly [1982] employed 45 subjects in a design in which expected values of each wager were not provided (his Group 1). Pooling over all 265 cases in which an ordinal preference was expressed in Parts 1 and 3, he reports (Table 2, p. 581) a preference reversal frequency of 41.9 percent.

---

[19] After my replication was conducted and analyzed, Charles Plott kindly provided the original GP data. Qualitatively identical results obtain from using the GP data as in my replication. I am also grateful to Robert Reilly for providing complete access to the (collated) data from Group 1 of his Stage 2 experiment.

We find that the foregone expected income of all of these decisions is a mere 0.644 cents per decision, averaging over all subjects. Of these costs, 80%, 93%, 96% and 100% of the subjects had average costs no greater than 1, 2, 3 and 4 cents, respectively.

There is one feature of the Reilly [1982] design that might bias the results in favour of observing low costs of misbehavior. Specifically, the increase in the buyout range for the BDM procedure from (0,999) to (−400,1400) has the unfortunate feature of reducing the monetary incentives that the subjects faced. Harrison [1992; Table 1, p. 1429] demonstrates that a subject with the GP buyout interval (0,999) would have to report selling prices of plus or minus 45, 64, 78, 90 or 100 cents in order to generate expected foregone incomes of 1, 2, 3, 4 or 5 cents, respectively. With the *expanded* buyout range the foregone expected income of these false reports *drops* to 0.550, 1.120, 1.668, 2.224 and 2.749 cents, respectively.

We can hypothetically evaluate the effect of expanding the buyout range on the cost of the observed subject behavior. This exercise provides some check that the non-dominance of payoffs in this experiment is not solely attributable to the expansion of the buyout range. Specifically, we simply set all reported valuations less than zero cents to zero and all reports greater than 999 cents to 999. The effect of this is to slightly increase the average cost of inconsistent valuations from 0.644 cents to 0.788 cents, pooling over all 45 subjects. Clearly this feature of the Reilly [1982] design, although unfortunate from the perspective of enhancing subject incentives, makes little difference to our conclusions.[20]

B The GP Replications

We have replicated the design of Experiment 1 of GP. Our procedures differ slightly, primarily due to the use of a microcomputer laboratory to undertake

[20] One feature of these preference reversal experiments that makes a major difference is the use of only one decision to reward subjects. As noted earlier, this implies that each costly decision has only a 1-in-18 chance of actually being costly. We can hypothetically evaluate the effect of this design feature by assuming that subjects were paid according to all of their decisions. This raises the average cost of "as if" preference reversals from 0.6444 cents to a serious 11.596 cents. We emphasize, however, that this thought-experiment is not the empirical experiment that these subjects were faced with. It is therefore a properly open behavioral question if they would report the same degree of "inconsistent" valuations if forced to live with the full costs of same.

Moreover, the earnings of subjects leap as one pays them for every decision. By stating selling prices of zero for all of the Part 2 decisions, for example, a subject could expect to earn $60 from the demand buyout (an average buyout of $5 time 12 decisions). On top of any earnings from Parts 1 and 2, this would make a foregone expected income of 11 cents seem trifling. This result raises an intriguing issue – what is the "appropriate" metric with which to evaluate the opportunity cost of an observed decision? Implicitly we have adopted throughout a metric of foregone income, measured simply in dollars and cents. However, in this setting it seems more appropriate to consider *percent* foregone income relative to the expected income at the optimal decision.

the experiment. All subjects were economics undergraduates at the University of Western Ontario.

Experiment *R1* employed 20 subjects with no monetary incentives to make good decisions: all subjects were paid a fixed amount just for participating. One variant of the GP procedure is that we played out the results of each decision after it was made, rather than selecting just one decision at the end of the experiment. The rate of observed preference reversals was 49%, somewhat higher than the 33% observed by GP (Table 5, p. 632). The hypothetical foregone expected income from these inconsistent choices was an average 18.3 cents per decision. These subjects hypothetically earned an average of $111 for the experiment, however.

Experiment *R2* employed 14 subjects with payoffs depending on just one of their decisions. The preference reversal rate was 45%, very close to the rate we observed in R1 for completely unmotivated subjects drawn form the same population. *The foregone expected income per inconsistent decision averaged only 0.6 cents!* We conclude that the subjects in these preference reversal experiments had virtually no incentive to behave any more consistently than they did.

C *Controlling for Payoff Dominance*

In an effort to increase the motivation of subjects we conducted an experiment with 13 subject facing the same design as *R2* but with a buyout range of (0,500) instead of (0,999). This constrains the selling prices that can be reported, but doubles the expected cost of a false report in this region. Moreover, the expected actuarial value of the GP wagers varies between $1.35 and $3.86, which is well within the truncated buyout interval. We observe a preference reversal rate of 46%, roughly as before. We also observe an average foregone expected income of only 0.5 cents, again as in experiment *R2*.

The Dominance problem arises in these experiments because of two factors. The first is the use of the BDM procedure for the elicitation of selling prices. For any given lottery, the elicited prices can be widely dispersed around the "true" certainty equivalent and the subject not forego significant amounts of expected income. The second factor is that the expected value of the paired lotteries are deliberately very similar. The expected values in the six pairs of GP [1979; Table 2, p. 629] differed by only 1, 7, 3, 6, 6, and 8 cents, respectively. The rationale for having lottery pairs with similar expected values, although not made explicit in GP, is to focus solely on the disparate effects of the elicitation devices (direct preference reports versus selling prices).

We designed an experiment to test the effect of controlling for payoff Dominance by varying the increment in selling prices that could be reported. The idea is to require the subject to state a selling price in increments of 25 cents, 50 cents, 100 cents or 200 cents, rather than the default increment of 1 cent. By doing this

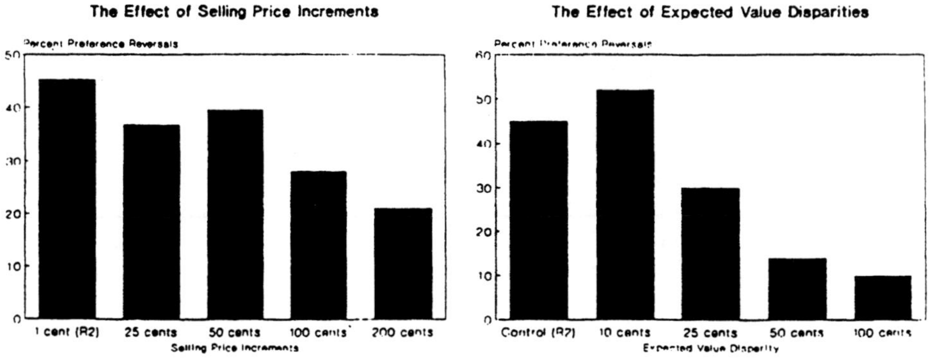

Fig. 5. Preference reversals

we reduce the accuracy of the report, but increase the opportunity cost of false reports. For example, an increment of 25 cents implies that a non-truthful report 25 cents either side of the true certainty-equivalent will have up to 25 times the probability of being costly for the subject. In each of these experiments we retained the original buyout range of (0,999).

The results presented in Figure 5 indicate a noticeable reduction in the rate of preference reversals using this treatment. Nonetheless, the payoff Dominance problem is not easily eradicated, even with this treatment. The average cost of "as if" preference reversals varies from 0.591 cents in our Control experiment *R2* to 0.777 cents, 0.716 cents, 0.417 cents, and 0.351 cents, respectively, for the experiments with increments of 25, 50, 100 and 200 cents. These experiments employed 19, 19, 19 and 15 subjects, respectively.

We also designed an experiment to test the effect of controlling for payoff Dominance by varying the expected value of the lottery pairs. If we make the disparity in expected values large enough for a given pair, then presumably the flatness of the payoff function with respect to selling prices will matter less and less. For example, assume that the subject is effectively indifferent between reports that are 25 cents either side of his true certainty-equivalent but is sensitive to the cost of large deviations. If the expected values of the lotteries are more than 50 cents apart then the selling prices elicited for each will generate the true ordinal preference even if they are "off" in terms of accurately representing the certainty-equivalent value. Moreover, if we assume that the opportunity cost of a non-truthful selling price increases monotonically from the true selling price, then as we steadily increase the disparity in expected values we should expect to see monotonically fewer preference reversals.

Admirable as this logic is, the calculations in Harrison [1992, Table 1, p. 1429] suggest that we may need to induce potentially huge differences in expected value in order to get a noticeable reduction in preference reversals. Using the example presented there, the subject could state selling pries in a $2.00 range around the true certainty-equivalent and still only forego an expected income of 5 cents.

Notwithstanding this pessimistic outlook, it seemed appropriate to venture into the laboratory and see if human subjects perceived things as outlined above – after all, experimental economics *is* an observational discipline. From Figure 5 it is apparent that they did not! The first treatment employed was to ensure that the expected values of each of the paired lotteries differed by 100 cents. In each of these experiments we employed a buyout range of (0,999), again wanting to focus solely on the effect of changing the expected values.[21] The preference reversal rate fell to only 10% over 25 subjects, compared to the 45% observed in experiment *R2* with 14 subjects drawn from the same population. Drunk with the brute simplicity of this observation, it seemed natural to see if smaller disparities in expected value would have a similar effect. Figure 5 shows that there is indeed a marked reduction in the rate of preference reversals for expected value disparities of 50 cents (over 13 subjects). The rate is somewhat higher when the disparity is only 25 cents (12 subjects), and is actually higher than in *R2* when the disparity is just 10 cents (12 subjects).

Nonetheless, the monotonic decline in the rate of preference reversals as the expected value disparity is increased from 25 cents up to 100 cents is consistent with our underlying hypothesis that the experimental evidence against EUT relies, in part, on a failure to control for payoff Dominance. The fact that a disparity of only 100 cents was sufficient to induce consistent behavior is somewhat surprising, but serves as a useful reminder that we are necessarily dealing with subjective and environment-specific costs of decision-making in experiments.

3 Prospect Theory

Kahneman and Tversky [1979] and Tversky and Kahneman [1986], hereafter generically KT and TK, catalogue a wide range of experimental anomalies from the perspective of EUT. To the extent that virtually all of these anomalies involve non-salient hypothetical questionnaires, one is tempted to dismiss them out of hand as not meeting the sufficient conditions for a valid microeconomics experiments. Two counter-arguments cause us to consider these anomalies more carefully, however. The first is the claim that these anomalies "persist even in the presence of significant monetary payoffs" (KT [1986; p. 90]; see also Thaler [1986; p. 96]). The second counter-argument is the fact that

[21] The expected values were changed by increasing the "win prize" in the P-bet of GP [1979; Table 2], except for pair 4 in which we lowered the value of "win prize". Consider pair 1, for example. The P-bet has a probability of winning of 35/36. To increase the expected value of the bet by ζ we simply increase the "win prize" by $\zeta/(35/36)$. Thus an increase in expected value of 100 cents requires an increase in the "win prize" of $103 \simeq 102.857$ cents.

these anomalies, and the Prospect Theory constructed to account for them, have achieved wide recognition and some respect amongst economists.

We evaluate the claim about the unimportance of monetary payoffs in two stages. First we re-examine those few experiments of KT and TK that did indeed use financial incentives, and that are heavily and repeatedly cited as support for the claim.[22] We find that the majority of these experiments do not satisfy the Dominance precept. Then we report the results of some new experiments designed to avoid our criticisms.

3.1 Some Old, But Salient, Experiments

A Salient Experiment 1

KT [1972] conducted one experiment with 97 Stanford undergraduates in which there were 3 questions. Each question defined a stochastic process (e.g., number of days in a year in which more boys than girls are born in a given hospital). The mean of this process is also specified (e.g., one-half of the days). A critical value above the mean is then introduced (e.g., number of days in which more than 60% of the babies born are boys). The subject is finally asked if this critical value is more likely to be observed in a small sample or a large sample (e.g., in a small hospital which has about 15 births per day or a larger hospital which has about 45 births per day).

The subjects were paid $1 if their answer to one of the three problems was correct. Thus the incentive to provide a correct answer on any given problem was 33 cents. Pooling over all three problems, 71% of the answers were incorrect. Viewing this proportion as representative of the likelihood that a given subject would give an incorrect answer, we see that such misbehavior leads to the subject foregoing an expected payoff of 0.71 (33 cents) = 23.6 cents per decision.

It should also be noted that KT gave the subject three possible answers. Two of these allowed an unambiguous choice of one or other of the samples (e.g., "The larger hospital", or "The smaller hospital"). The third allowed for a rough indifference to be expressed: viz., "About the same (i.e., within 5% of each other)". This approximate indifference option was chosen in 47% of all answers, and may indicate subject confusion or disinterest. If we disregard such choices, the foregone expected payoff from unambiguous errors drops to (70/152) 33 = 15.2 cents per decision. KT do not say how long this experimental session lasted.

[22] Undoubtedly there are several other experiments conducted with financial incentives that we have overlooked. Nonetheless, the general message should be quite clear from the sample we do consider. Harrsion [1992;p.1430] evaluates one further salient experiment by TK [1986; pp. 80–81].

B Salient Experiment 2

TK [1973] conducted one experiment with 50 Stanford undergraduates which involves them considering the following diagram:

x x 0 x x x
x x x x 0 x
x 0 x x x x
x x x 0 x x
x x x x x 0
0 x x x x x

A path was defined for the subject as "any descending line which starts at the top row, ends at the bottom row, and passes through exactly one symbol (x or 0) in each row". Subjects were simply asked if they thought that there are more paths connecting six x's and no 0 or more paths connecting five x's and one 0. Each subject received $1 for a correct answer and zero payoff for an incorrect answer.

The distribution of paths is "well-known", to combinatorial theorists presumably, as being binominal with $p = 5/6$ and $n = 6$. Thus about 33% of the paths consists of six x's, and about 40% of the paths consists of exactly five x's. Hence the correct answer is that there are more paths consisting of exactly five x's. The proportion of paths that consists of exactly 4, 3, 2, 1 or 0 x's is each significantly lower than either of these two (around 20% for exactly 4 x's, and below 6% for each of the other paths).

Each subject was rewarded with $1 if he gave a correct answer. Nonetheless, 38 of the subjects gave the wrong answer. Viewing these as responses from a homogenous sample, a subject is therefore likely to make a mistake with 0.76 probability, implying a foregone expected payoff (due to this likelihood of mistake) of 76 cents. Relative to the extraordinary computational difficulty of the task this is not a large payoff.[23] Again, TK do not say how much time the subjects were given to respond to the question.

C Salient Experiment 3

TK [1981] posed 3 simple stochastic choice questions to a single group of subjects and gave one-tenth of each group the opportunity to play the gamble

[23] Smith [1982; p. 934, fn. 17] correctly points out that the Dominance requirement for a given (cognitive or computational) task should be defined relative to the availability of (perceptual or calculating) aids. Did these subjects have pen and paper available? Did they have pocket calculators? Were there any implicit or explicit time limits on their answers?

they chose. These questions were as follows, with the percent of subjects choosing each option reported in square brackets:

1) Choose between (*A*) a sure gain of $30 [78%], and (*B*) 80% chance to win $45 and 20% chance to win nothing [22%];
2) Choose between (*C*) 25% chance to win $30 and 75% to win nothing [42%], and (*D*) 20% chance to win $45 and 80% chance to win nothing [58%]; and
3) Consider the following two stage game. In the first stage, there is a 75% chance to end the game without winning anything, and a 25% chance to move into the second stage. If you reach the second stage you have a choice between (*E*) a sure win of $30 [74%], and (*F*) 80% chance to win $45 and 20% chance to win nothing [26%].

Problems (2) and (3) are identical in EUT terms, and problem (2) is a simple positive affine transformation of problem (1). Hence a preference for *A* over *B* implies a preference for *C* over *D* and for *E* over *F*, according to EUT.

Assume that the observed choices refer to a homogenous pool of risk-neutral agents, so that we can think of the responses as coming from one representative agent rather than the sample of 85 subjects. The expected value of each lottery is readily calculated as: (*A*) $30, (*B*) $36, (*C*) $7.50, (*D*) $9, (*E*) $7.50 and (*F*) $9.

How costly was it for our representative subject to behave as observed? By only reporting a preference for *B* over *A* with probability 0.22 (instead of with probability 1), he foregoes $(1 - 0.22)((36 - 30) \div 10) = \$0.468$. By only reporting a preference for *D* over *C* with probability 0.58, he foregoes $(1 - 0.58)((9.00 - 7.50) \div 10) = \$0.063$. Similarly, he foregoes $0.111 in problem (3). Thus the total response pattern for all three questions implies a foregone expected income to a risk neutral agent of $0.468 + 0.063 + 0.111 = \$0.642$.

Given the clear pattern of preferences in questions (1) and (3), and the lack of a clear preference pattern in question (2), it seems more natural to assume that our representative agent is risk averse. Let us assume further that the certainty-equivalent income required to compensate for the riskiness of prospect *B* is $6 (plus ε). Thus our agent foregoes $0.22(6 \div 10) = \$0.132$ by reporting a preference for B over A with probability 0.22 (instead of with zero probability). Similarly, he foregoes $0.58(1.50 \div 10) = \$0.087$ and $0.26(1.50 \div 10) = \$0.039$ in problems (2) and (3) by stating a preference for the prospect that is more risky with probability 0.58 and 0.26, respectively. Thus a risk averse agent foregoes as little as $0.132 + 0.087 + 0.039 = \$0.258$. This is clearly a lower bound, since we assume the least possible certainty-equivalent such that the preference under EUT would not be for *B* over *A*.

We conclude that a representative subject who behaved in the probabilistic pattern observed would, under plausible enough assumptions, have foregone between 26 cents and 47 cents.

D Salient Experiment 4

TK [1983; p. 303] devise an experiment to illustrate "the conjunction fallacy". This is a phenomenon involving two probabilistic events, A and B. The subject is asked, in effect, whether "A" or "A and B" are more likely. Sadly for EUT they tend to select the latter. Consider the following instructions:

Consider a regular six-sided die with four green faces and two red faces. The die will be rolled 20 times and the sequence of greens (G) and reds (R) will be recorded. You are asked to select one sequence, from a set of three, and you will win $25 if the sequence you chose appears on successive rolls of the die. Please check the sequence of greens and reds on which you prefer to bet.

1. RGRRR
2. GRGRRR
3. GRRRRR

The subjects were 260 undergraduates at UBC and Stanford, with 125 of them playing out the gamble as stated in the instructions (one presumes that an oral addition to these instructions alert subjects in the hypothetical payment to the fact that their decisions are not salient). Sequence 1 corresponds to event A, and "a G at the beginning of the sequence" corresponds to event B, hence sequence 2 corresponds to the conjunction of A and B. The subjects facing monetary payoffs chose sequence 1, 2 and 3 in 33%, 65% and 29% of the observed choices. The choice pattern for the other subjects was virtually identical.

The exact probability of each sequence occurring in a 20-trial sequence is messy to calculate. A close approximation can be obtained by asking what the probability is of observing sequence 1 in any 5 rolls of the die ($= \frac{1}{3}\cdot\frac{2}{3}\cdot\frac{1}{3}\cdot\frac{1}{3}\cdot\frac{1}{3} =$ 0.0082304), of observing sequence 2 in any 6 rolls ($= 0.0082304\cdot\frac{2}{3} = 0.0054869$), and of observing sequence 3 in any 6 rolls ($= 0.0027434$). With a $25 prize, the expected value of choosing sequence 1, 2 or 3 is 20.576 cents, 13.717 cents and 6.858 cents, respectively. By choosing sequence 2 over sequence 1 a risk neutral subject forgoes only 6.859 cents. If we again think of the observed frequency of choices as representing the probability of a given (representative) subject choosing sequence 2 or 3 over sequence 1, we find that the opportunity cost of the sub-optimal behavior is $0.65(6.859) + 0.02(13.718) = 4.458 + 0.274 = 4.732$. Again, relative to the extraordinary computational difficulty of the decision facing the subject, this is not a particularly costly error.

3.2 Some New Experiments

A large number of the choice anomalies presented by KT rest on a failure of the axiom of EUT that states that if $B \succ A$ then $(B; p) \succ (A; p)$ for any probability

p, where $(X; q)$ denotes a (possibly compound) lottery in which X is received with probability q. Consider, for example, Problems 7 and 8 of KT [1979; p. 267]. The subject is asked to choose between A: (6000;0.45) and B: (3000;0.90), and 86% of their subjects chose prospect B. The subject is separately asked to choose between C: (6000;0.001) and D: (3000;0.002), and 73% of the subjects chose C. Clearly C is just the compound lottery (A;1/450) and D the compound lottery (B;1/450). EUT predicts that the subjects should choose D over C, but the modal choice pattern of this subject pool is the reverse of this.[24]

In order to focus on the question of payoff Dominance we have conducted a series of Salient experiments in which subjects were presented with a number of

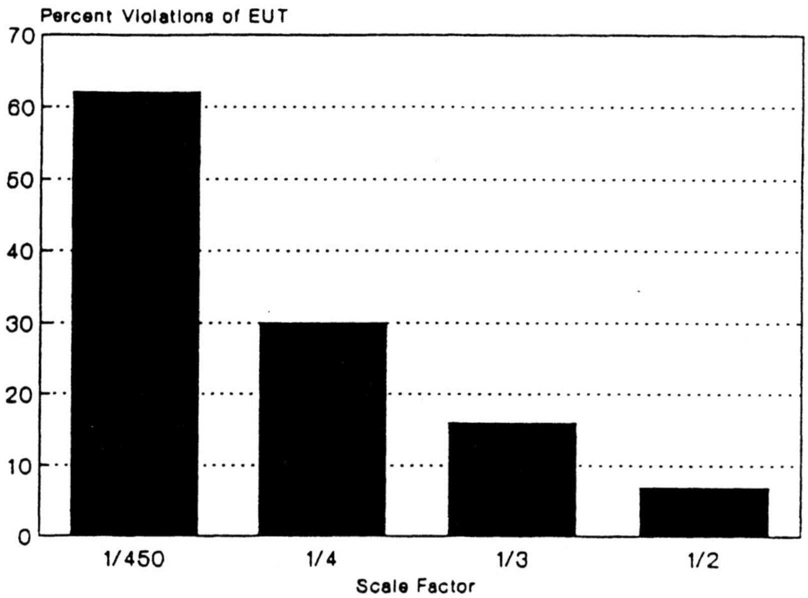

Fig. 6. Tests of EUT in simple pairwise lottery choices

[24] One frustrating aspect of the reporting style of KT is that they do not typically report the pattern of choices in paired decision problems. In this example we would like to know the percentage of subjects that chose B over A and *then* chose C over D, violating EUT. Given that 14% of the subjects chose A over B and 73% chose C over D, it is possible that all of the subjects in this 14% behaved consistently with EUT and chose C, so that the percentage of subjects violating EUT is only 73% − 14% = 59%. This is still, of course, likely to be significantly greater than zero, but it is a more meaningful measure of the performance of EUT. It should also be noted that although KT [1979; p. 266] report when a preference is "significant at the .01 level" they do not tell us the null or alternative hypotheses, let alone the statistical procedure used. Their classification of the significance of their results is consistent with a χ^2 test of a null of equi-probable choices against a two-sided alternative. Note that these tests appear to have been performed for the pairwise choice, not for the pattern of choices predicted by EUT.

pairwise choice problems of this kind. We vary the "scale factor" p in these problems so as to evaluate behaviorally the trade-off between payoff Dominance and violations of EUT. To see why this is important, consider the expected value of the above prospects for a risk neutral subject, presuming that "6000" refers to "6000 cents". Lotteries A and B have an expected value of \$2.70, whereas C and D only have an expected value of \$0.01! Thus if a strict preference over A and B is based on some attitude to risk, so must any preference defined over C and D. However, any differences in the certainty-equivalents of the lottery pairs A and B must be miniscule for the lottery pairs C and D for plausible attitudes to risk. The upshot of this is that if we consider a range of values of the "scale factor" p we should be able to capture an effect from varying the extent of payoff Dominance.

Figure 6 displays the results of our experiments, conducted with 50 undergraduate economics students from the University of Western Ontario. The monetary prizes used were C\$6.00 and C\$3.00 as above. The "scale factor" p was set equal to a range of values, 1/450, 1/4, 1/3 and 1/2. Each subject faced the five choices in a random sequence. The results are very clear. As the payoff Dominance problem is reduced, by increasing the value of p, the extent of violations of EUT declines dramatically. Note that we observe 62% of all choices for the $p = 1/450$ problems were inconsistent with EUT, which is a result comparable to KT [1979]. This indicates that, unlike the Allais Paradox considered earlier, the pure effect of Salient payoffs is not sufficient to ensure consistent choice behavior. Rather, one must also ensure that the payoffs for the decision problem satisfy Dominance.

4. Bayes Rule

4.1 The Experiment

The most influential study on the extent to which agents use Bayes Rule in making statistical inferences has been Grether [1980]. He devised a classic experiment to test the hypothesis that subjects behave as if they follow Bayes Rule in a simple statistical inference problem.[25] One alternative hypothesis, advocated by KT [1972], is that agents use a Representativeness Heuristic in such problems which will tend to bias their inferences relative to the prediction derived from following Bayes Rule. This Heuristic essentially holds that subjects

---

[25] A number of studies have extended this test of Bayes Rule to market environments: see Anderson and Sunder [1988], Camerer [1987] and Duh and Sunder [1986].

will evaluate the probability of a sample according to the population process that it most closely "represents". From a Bayesian perspective it is as if such subjects attach too little weight to prior probabilities and too much weight to sample evidence. With non-diffuse priors this will lead to systematic departures from Bayes Rule.

Grether [1980; p. 540] correctly notes three major problems with the experiments that the psychologists claim support this Heuristic. First, the inferential problem itself involved highly subjective verbal situations which subjects might not know how to operationalize. Second, there may have been some incredibility with respect to the random processes that were described to the subjects: the Peterson and Ulehla [1965] binary choice experiments are a celebrated example of this effect. Finally, the psychology experiments were not Salient.

The experimental design proposed by Grether [1980] nicely eliminates these problems. The instructions that our subjects received, in a replication of his design, succinctly describe the task:

> The experimenters are trying to determine how people make decisions. We have designed a simple choice experiment, and we shall ask you to make decisions at various times. The amount of money you make will depend on how good your decisions are. During the experiment you will be asked to make ten decisions. At the end of the experiment we shall randomly choose one of your ten decisions and give you $10 if it is correct. If it is incorrect you will receive $1. [In treatment B2 the previous 2 sentences were replaced with: If a decision is correct you will receive $1.00. If it is incorrect you will only receive $0.10. Therefore, if you make ten correct decisions you will earn $10.00.] We shall then repeat the experiment for another ten decisions, with the same rules. [In treatment B0 the previous 5 sentences were replaced with: You will receive $2.50 for making these decisions. During the experiment you will be asked to make ten decisions. We shall then repeat the experiment for another ten decisions, with the same rules. You will receive $2.50 for each set of ten decisions ($5 for all twenty decisions).]
>
> The computer is going to use three randomizing devices in this experiment, which you can think of as bingo cages designated as CAGE A, CAGE B, and CAGE X. Inside both CAGE A and CAGE B are six balls, some of which are marked with an N and some with a G. CAGE A has four N's and 2 G's and CAGE B has three N's and 3 G's. Inside CAGE X there are six balls numbered one, two, three, four, five, and six.
>
> The experiment will proceed as follows. First, the computer will spin CAGE X. Before each run we will tell you that if certain numbers come up, we will choose CAGE A, and otherwise we will choose CAGE B. For example, if 1, 2, 3 or 4 are drawn, we will pick CAGE A; if a 5 or 6 is drawn, we will pick CAGE B. After drawing from CAGE X, the computer will choose the appropriate CAGE (A or B). Then the computer will make six draws from the CAGE that has been selected, replacing the drawn ball each time. You will be told the results of the draws by the computer. You will then be asked to indicate (to the computer, and in writing on your Record Sheet) whether you think the draws come from CAGE A or CAGE B.
>
> The only talking allowed during the course of the experiment will be to clarify questions you may have about the procedure, and these questions should be directed to the experimenter. The computer will now take you through a trial decision to make sure that you understand the procedure. This decision (Decision 0) will not be used to determine your payoffs.

These instructions vary slightly from those used by Grether [1980; p. 555–6], primarily with respect to the use of a microcomputer to conduct the experiment. The only problem that this variation may have generated is the credibility of the

Table 2. Parameters and expected payoffs in Bayes rule experiment

Prior Probability of Cage *A*	Number of N's in sample... 0	1	2	3	4	5	6
			(a) Posterior Probability of Cage *A*				
.67	.149	.260	.413**	.584**	.737	.849	.918
.5	.081	.149	.260	.413***	.584***	.737	.849
.33	.042	.081	.149	.260	.413*	.584**	.737
			(b) Correct Decision				
.67	B	B	B**	A*	A	A	A
.5	B	B	B	B***	A***	A	A
.33	B	B	B	B	B*	A**	A
			(c) Expected Payoffs for Correct Decision (Grether Design; in U.S. cents)				
.67	42.7	29.2	10.6**	10.2*	28.8	42.4	50.8
.5	50.9	42.7	29.2	10.6***	10.2***	28.8	42.4
.33	55.7	50.9	42.7	29.2	10.6*	10.2*	28.8
			(d) Expected Payoffs for Correct Decision (Current Design; in Canadian cents)				
.67	63.2	43.2	15.7**	15.1*	42.7	62.8	75.2
.5	75.4	63.2	43.2	15.7***	15.1***	42.7	62.8
.33	82.4	75.4	63.2	43.2	15.7*	15.1**	42.7

Note: Recall that Cage *A* has 4 N's and Cage *B* has 3 N's.

random process[26], although if this effect is systematic it will bias results away from the null hypothesis (Bayes Rule).

Table 2 shows the parameters and expected payoffs in our experiment. Panels (a) and (b) compute the posterior probability of Cage A generating each possible sample as a function of the prior and the observed sample. Those entries with one or more asterisks all have approximately the same posterior probability favouring the correct decision according to Bayes Rule. However, those cells with exactly one asterisk are instances in which the Representativeness Heuristic would lead a subject to make the incorrect decision: with 3 N's the Heuristic implies that the population would be Cage B, and with 4 N's it would be Cage A. In each case there are specific priors that would overshadow this sample evidence. Cells with two asterisks are instances in which the Heuristic would favor neither choice, and three asterisks denote cells in which the Heuristic favors the correct decision. The attractive feature of this design is that the predictions of the two hypotheses differ sharply for a set of possible out-

[26] Having the computer draw the sample may also have made it difficult for subjects to operationalize the random process. Hence the instructions contain liberal references to the idea that the subject could think of these drawings as if they had come from an urn (the physical process employed by Grether [1980]).

comes that hold constant the strength of the incentives for one of the hypotheses (the null, Bayes Rule).

Three financial incentive structures were employed. The first was to pay subjects a fixed amount for making a certain number of decisions (C$3 in our experiment). The second was to pay subjects for one of their decisions. The third was to pay subjects for each decision. In each case we revealed the true Cage generating the sample after each decision.

Each subject was asked to make 20 decisions. These were divided into two groups of ten, with any earnings tallied at the end of each set of ten decisions. In terms of the information about total earnings revealed to subjects the first and second set of ten decisions correspond to the usual notions of "inexperienced subject behavior" and "experienced subject behavior", respectively. Grether [1980] conducted one session with his subjects, lasting an average of 16.45 periods.[27] He employs a non-standard definition of "experience" when analysing his results: he calls a given subject's decision an experienced one if the subject had previously been exposed to the same prior-sample cell in panel (a) of Table 2. There is nothing "wrong" with this definition, but it does differ from the standard experimental notion of an experienced subject as one who has participated in the entire experiment before.

The reason that the precise notion of "subject experience" is of concern here is that one of the most important and often cited conclusions from Grether [1980] is that subjects do tend to follow the Heuristic instead of Bayes Rule, and that "monetary incentives do not appear to affect the behavior of inexperienced subjects (...) This is not true, however, for the experienced subjects." (p. 552). His results suggest that a combination of experience and monetary incentives only makes the case for Bayes Rule having a strong effect on the probability that a subject will make the correct choice (see his Table 4).

Finally, consider the question of the level of payoffs. Grether [1980] paid the subjects in his Fixed incentives sessions US$7; ours were paid C$3 for each set of 10 decisions in treatment B0. In his One-Shot sessions Grether [1980] rewarded subjects with US$15 if they chose the correct cage in the decision selected for payment, and US$5 if they chose incorrectly. These incentives imply the expected payoffs for a correct decision in Panel (c) of Table 2. In order to have roughly comparable payoffs, after allowing for the U.S.-Canada exchange rate (approximately US$1 = C$1.3 at the time of the experiments), our One-Shot treatment B1 effectively used C$10 and C$1 for rewards. In the Multiple Reinforcement treatment B2 our subjects received C$1 per correct decision and C$0.10 (in effect) per incorrect decision. Thus the overall expected payoff for a correct decision was the same between treatments B1 and B2 (ignoring income effects).

[27] Grether [1980] does not say how many decisions were conducted in each of his 7 sessions. The average number is derived from the reported total number of subjects (341, on p. 541) and decisions (5608, in Table V on p. 550).

The substantive questions that motivated this 3×2 design were twofold. First, does "experience" as normally defined in the experimental literature influence the extent of the bias in decision-making predicted by the Heuristic? Answers to this question will come from an orthogonal comparison of behavior for a given payment method. The second question, prompted by the Saliency and Dominance precepts, is whether the provision of financial incentives in (three) different ways lowers the opportunity cost (i.e., foregone expected income) of sub-optimal decisions. That is, do we observe subjects making less costly errors if they face financial incentives not to do so?[28] Prompted by some remarks by Holt [1986b], the present design operationalizes "financial incentives" in three distinct ways: Fixed (non-marginal) incentives, One-Shot incentives and Multiple Reinforcement incentives.

All subjects were drawn from the economics undergraduate program at the University of Western Ontario. Each subject received C$2 for just showing up at the appointed time. This $2 payment served the double function of providing the reward for incorrect decisions referred to above.[29] Fourteen, twenty and sixteen subjects participated in treatments B0, B1 and B2, respectively.

4.2 *Inferences from the Experiment*

The results on the direct comparison of Bayes Rule and the Representativeness Heuristic are shown in Table 3. We observe clear evidence that the Heuristic strongly influences the propensity of unmotivated and inexperienced subjects to make correct decisions. The percent of such decisions that were correct is only 32% when the Heuristic favors the wrong choice, but it is 65% when the Heuristic reinforces the correct choice and it is precisely 50% when the Heuristic provides no guidance.[30] However, when these unmotivated and experienced subjects tackle the same class of problems[31] the Heuristic has no noticeable

---

[28] In a trivial sense no subject can make any costly errors in treatment B0! We evaluate the cost of errors in these experiments as if the subject had foregone payoffs such as applied in treatments B1 and B2. We will simply refer to the "cost of errors" in B0, rather than the more accurate "cost of hypothetical errors".

[29] Thus a subject in session B1 was told that a correct decision would earn him an additional C$10 and that he would not earn any additional payoff if his decision was incorrect. Whether or not one interprets the $2 as a show-up reward or a reward for incorrect decisions has no effect on the marginal incentive for correct decisions.

[30] All of our claims concerning the results from treatment B0 are statistically significant at standard confidence levels using non-parametric Kolmogorov-Smirnov test procedures (as implemented numerically from Press, Flannery, Teukolsky and Vetterling [1986]).

[31] The subjects did not face the same random sequence of prior-outcome combinations in their "inexperienced" and "experienced" sets of decisions. The random processes were re-seeded for each separate decision.

Table 3. Percent correct decisions in Bayes rule experiments

Experiment	Payment Method	Experienced Subjects?	Representativeness Heuristic Favors...		
			Wrong Choice	Neither Choice	Correct Choice
Grether	*Fixed*	No	54	74	84
	One-Shot	No	61	80	82
B0	*Fixed*	No	32	50	65
		Yes	63	62	59
B1	*One-Shot*	No	43	54	50
		Yes	42	33	43
B2	*Multiple*	No	50	44	55
		Yes	39	38	39

Note: These percentages only refer to the six decisions which have roughly the same posterior odds in favor of the correct decision and which test the representativeness heuristic (those with one or more asterisks in Table 2).

influence at all. The propensity of such subjects to make correct decisions is about 60% irrespective of the disparate predictions based on the Heuristic.

The influence of the Heuristic is weak when inexperienced subjects facing One-Shot motivation make their decisions, and nonexistent when these subjects are experienced. Finally, there is no evidence whatsoever for the Heuristic when subjects with Multiple Reinforcement motivation make decisions. This final conclusion is true irrespective of the experience level of the subjects.

4.3 *The Cost of Misbehavior*

Table 4 shows the percentage distribution of the costs of sub-optimal decisions for each experiment and experience level. In all six cases the distribution is heavily skewed with a median cost of zero cents. The average costs are 11.2, 11.1 and 11.0 cents for inexperienced subjects in B0, B1 and B2, respectively, and 11.5, 10.0 and 8.6 cents for experienced subjects. Given the skewness of these distributions, it should be emphasized that the median is a better descriptive statistic than the mean as a measure of central tendency.

We therefore conclude that our experiments show that there is no evidence against Bayes Rule when subjects are experienced or face repetitive financial motivation. Moreover, any deviations from Bayes Rule tended to be virtually costless ones, irrespective of the experience level or type of financial incentives used.

Table 4. Costliness of decisions in Bayes rule experiments

Expected Cost in Cents	Experience Level	*B0*	*B1*	*B2*
0	Inexperienced	62%	65%	63%
	Experienced	61	68	72
15–16	Inexperienced	23	19	20
	Experienced	20	19	16
42–44	Inexperienced	9	13	13
	Experienced	15	9	8
62–64	Inexperienced	6	4	4
	Experienced	3	5	4
≥75	Inexperienced	0	1	1
	Experienced	0	1	0

5 Conclusions

It may appear that our tone has been overly defensive, even polemical, in support of the received theory of choice under uncertainty. That may be so, but some perspective on the monolithic acceptance of the reported experimental anomalies may justify such a position. For example, Zeckhauser [1986; p. 254] proposes as an "obvious" and "untestable" axiom that for "... any rational choice, the behavioralists (e.g., Amos Tversky) can produce a laboratory counter-example." We disagree with this view. Our review of several of the most widely cited pieces of experimental evidence contrary to EUT and Bayes Rule leads to the conclusion that they do not satisfy the accepted precepts of experimental economics. Moreover, modifications to the experiments to remedy these design weaknesses results in observed choice behavior consistent with the predictions of economic theory.

References

Allais M (1979) Le comportement de l'homme rationnel devant le risque: Critique des postulats et axiomes de l'Ecole Americaine. Econometrica 21:1953, 503–546; English translation in Allais M, Hagen O (eds) Expected utility hypotheses and the allais paradox

Battalio RC, Kagel JH, Jiranyakul K (1990) Testing between alternative models of choice under uncertainty: Some initial results. Journal of Risk and Uncertainty 3:25–50

Becker GM, DeGroot MH, Marschak J (1964) Measuring utility by a single-response sequential method. Behavioral Science 9:226–232

Berg JE, Daley LA, Dickhaut JW, O'Brien JR (1986) Controlling preferences for lotteries on units of experimental exchange. Quarterly Journal of Economics 101:281–306

Camerer CF (1987) Do biases in probability judgement matter in markets? Experimental evidence. American Economic Review 77:981–997

Camerer CF (1989) An experimental test of several generalized expected utility theories. Journal of Risk and Uncertainty 2:61–104

Chew SH, Waller WS (1986) Empirical tests of weighted utility theory. Journal of Mathematical Psychology 30:55–72

Conlisk J (1989) Three variants on the allais example. American Economic Review 79:392–407

Conover WJ (1980) Practical nonparametric statistics. New York Wiley, Second Edition

Cox JC, Epstein S (1989) Preference reversals without the independence axiom. American Economic Review 79:408–426

Davis DD, Holt CA (1993) Experimental economics. Princeton Princeton University Press

Duh RR, Sunder S (1986) Incentives, learning, and processing of information in a market environment: An ecaminatio of the base rate fallacy. In: Moriarty S (ed) Laboratory Market Research. Norman OK University of Oklahoma Press.

Forsythe R, Palfrey TR, Plott CR (1982) Asset Valuation in an experimental market. Econometrica 50:537–582

Grether DM (1980) Bayes rule as a descriptive model: The representativeness heuristic. Quarterly Journal of Economics 95:537–557

Grether DM, Plott CR (1979) Economic theory of choice and the preference reversal phenomenon. American Economic Review 69:623–638

Grether DM, Plott CR (1982) Economic theory of choice and the preference reversal phenomenon: Reply. American Economic Review 72:575

Harrison GW Theory and misbehavior of first-price auctions. American Economic Review 79: 749–762

Harrison GW (1992) Theory and misbehavior of first-price auctions: Reply. American Economic Review 82:1426–1443

Harrison GW, Morgan PB (1990) Search intensity in experiments. Economic Journal 100:478–486

Hey JD, Di Cagno D (1990) Circles and triangles: An experimental estimation of indifference lines in the marschak-machina triangle. Journal of Behavioral Decision Making 3:279–306

Holt, CA (1986a) The independence axiom and preference reversals. American Economic Review 76:508–513

Holt CA (1986b) Discussant's comments In: Moriarty S (ed.). Laboratory Market Research. Norman OK University of Oklahoma Press

Kahneman D, Tversky (1972) Subjective probability: A judgement of representitiveness. Cognitive Psychology 3:430–454

Kahneman D, Tversky A (1973) On the psychology of prediction. Psychological Review 84:237–251

Kahneman D, Tversky A (1978) Prospect theory: An analysis of decision under risk. Econometrica 47:263–291

Karni E, Safra Z (1987) Preference reversals' and the observability of preferences by experimental methods. Econometrica 55:675–685

Leamer EE, Leonard HB (1983) Reporting the fragility of regression estimates. Review of Economics and Statistics 65:306–317

Loomes G, Sugden R (1983) A rationale for preference reversal. American Economic Review 73: 428–432

Machina MJ (1982) Expected utility analysis without the independence axiom. Econometrica 50: 277–323

Machina MJ (1987) Choice under uncertainty: Problems solved and unsolved. Journal of Economic Perspectives 1:121–154

Mosteller F, Nogee P (1951) An experimental measurement of utility. Journal of Political Economy 59:371–404

Peterson CR, Ulehla ZJ (1965) Sequential patterns and maximizing. Journal of Experimental Psychology 69:1–4

Plott CR, Sunder S (1982) Efficiency of experimental security markets with insider information: An application of rational-expectations models. Journal of Political Economy 90:663–698

Pommerehne WW, Schneider F, Zweifel P, (1982) Economic theory of choice and the preference reversal phenomenon: A reexamination. American Economic Review 72:569–574

Press WH, Flannery BP, Teukolsky SA, Vetterling WA (1986) Numerical recipes: The art of scientific computing. Cambridge University Press

Reilly RJ (1982) Preference reversal: Further evidence and some suggested modifications in experimental design. American Economic Review 72:576–584

Roth AE (1988) Laboratory experimentation in economics: A methodological overview. Economic Journal 89:974–1031

Roth AE, Malouf MWK (1979) Game-theoretic models and the role of information in bargaining. Psychological Review 86:574–594

Segal U (1988) Does the preference reversal phenomenon necessarily contradict the independence axiom? American Economic Review 78:233–236

Starmer C, Sugden R (1991) Does the random-lottery incentive system elicit true preferences? An experimental investigation. American Economic Review 81:971–978

Thaler RH (1986) The psychology and economics conference handbook: Comments on simon, on einhorn and hogarth, and on tversky and kahneman. In: Hogarth RM, Reder MW (eds) Rational Choice. Chicago University of Chicago Press

Tversky A, Kahneman D (1971) Belief in the law of small numbers. Psychological Bulletin 76: 1105–1110

Tversky A, Kahneman D (1973) Availability: A heuristic for judging frequency and probability. Cognitive Psychology 5:207–232

Tversky A, Kahneman D (1981) The framing of decisions and the psychology of choice. Science 211:453–458

Tversky A, Kahneman D (1983) Extensional versus intutive reasoning: The conjunction fallacy in probability judgement. Psychological Review 90:293–315

Tversky A, Kahneman D (1986) Rational choice and the framing of decisions. In: Hogarth RM, Reder MW (eds) Rational Choice. Chicago University of Chicage Press

Zeckhauser R (1986) Comments: Behavioral versus rational economics: What you see is what you conquer In: Hogarth RM, Reder MW (eds) Rational Choice. Chicago University of Chicago Press

Stationary Solution to the Overlapping Generations Model of Fiat Money: Experimental Evidence[1]

SUK S. LIM

City University of Seoul, Seoul, Korea

EDWARD C. PRESCOTT

Department of Economics, University of Minnesota, Minneapolis MN 55455, USA

SHYAM SUNDER

Graduate School of Industrial Administration, Carnegie Mellon University, Schenley Park, Pittsburgh PA 15213, USA

Abstract: Overlapping generations model of fiat money yields an infinity of competitive equilibrium solutions, only one of which is stationary. Economies reported in this paper involved a sequence of overlapping generations of three or four individuals; each individual lived for two periods. In their young age individuals were endowed with "chips" that could be traded for fiat money with the individuals of the old generation. In their old age, individuals could exchange their units of fiat money for the consumption good. Results of the experiments exhibit some support for the stationary solution. The results are robust to two designs of exchange institutions (double oral auction and supply schedule auction) and to two different endogenous ways of converting money into "chips" at the end of the game (average price prevailing during the last period the game is actually played and the average price forecast made during the last period the game is actually played).

JEL-Classification System-Numbers: C62, C92, E40, E50

The overlapping generations economy of Samuelson (1958) has become a central construct in monetary economics.[2] Lucas (1972), adding informationally decentralized exchange, used it to construct a monetary shock theory of business cycles. Since then a problem with using this abstraction has been recognized. There typically are not only the equilibria considered by Lucas but many others as well. Calvo (1978) showed there typically are a continuum of deterministic nonstationary equilibria. Azariadis (1982) and Cass and Shell (1984) found a set of sunspot equilibria. Kehoe and Levine (1985) showed that the problem of multiplicity of equilibria increases with the number of goods. Spear and Srivastava (1985) have constructed overlapping generations models with a continuum of stationary equilibria.

---

1 A preliminary version of this paper was presented at the meeting of the Economic Science Association and at the Federal Reserve Bank of Minneapolis. The authors are grateful for comments received from various participants at both presentations. Financial support was provided by the McKnight Foundation, the Honeywell Foundation, National Science Foundation (SES 89–12552), and Richard. M. and Margaret Cyert Family Funds.

2 Wallace (1980) has championed its use in addressing monetary issues.

The basic problem is that there are many consistent sets of expectations for the future price path. Competitive equilibrium theory alone cannot resolve the issue of which of the equilibrium paths is to be expected in a given economy. Lucas (1986) suggested the experimental approach to resolve this issue. If experimental economies converge to stationary nonsunspot equilibrium, such results would provide justification for focusing attention on this equilibrium. If the allocation obtained over experiments varies, the experimental results provide support for those who see policy as the choice of monetary arrangement (e.g., Grandmont, 1986). Often there are monetary institutions that can be adopted to eliminate the indeterminacy resulting in but one equilibrium with valued fiat money.

A key experimental innovation is overcoming the endpoint problem. For any finite-lived economy there are no monetary equilibria.[3] Money has no value at the last trading date because it cannot be traded for anything subsequently. If it has no value at the last trading date, it has no value at the date before. By induction, it has no value in any period. Consequently, there can be no last period in an economy designed to examine the equilibrium value of fiat money. But experimental economies necessarily have a last period. Our resolution of this problem is to add economic forecasters to the economy. The value of money in the last period of the experiment is the average value forecasted for that period in the period before by nonparticipating subjects who are rewarded for accuracy of their forecasts. For this environment, the same set of equilibria is obtained as for the infinitely lived economy in the sense that the paths are the same for the life of the infinite-lived economy.

The Economy

Consider a sequence of generations, each consisting of an equal number, n, of agents. Each agent lives over two consecutive periods $\{t, t+1\}$ and consumes y_t at the end of the first period (youth) and z_{t+1} at the end of the second (old age). Each agent is endowed with e_y units of a consumption good at the beginning of the youth period and e_z units at the beginning of the old age period and e_y exceeds e_z. The economy has $n \cdot m$ units of fiat money (i.e., m units per person) which can be used by the old to buy the good from the young each period. If each individual's preferences are given by $u\ (y_t, z_{t+1})$, the utility maximization problem can be specified as:

$$\max_{y_t, z_{t+1}, m_t} \ u(y_t, z_{t+1})$$

$$\text{subject to } m_t = (e_y - y_t)p_t$$

$$z_{t+1} = e_z + m_t/(p_{t+1})$$

[3] There is always a nonmonetary equilibrium in which there are no trades and fiat currency is not valued.

where p_t and p_{t+1} are the prices per unit of the good and m_t is the amount of money the individual acquires in youth and spends in the old age.

Substituting for y_t and z_{t+1}, the maximization problem can be written as:

$$\max_{m_t} u\left(e_y - \frac{m_t}{p_t}, e_z + \frac{m_t}{p_{t+1}}\right)$$

Assuming $u(y_t, z_{t+1}) = (y_t \cdot z_{t+1})$,

$$\max_{m_t} \left[\left(e_y - \frac{m_t}{p_t}\right)\left(e_z + \frac{m_t}{p_{t+1}}\right)\right].$$

First order condition is sufficient for optimization of this concave problem:

$$\left(e_z + \frac{m_t}{p_{t+1}}\right)\Big/ p_t = \left(e_y - \frac{m_t}{p_t}\right)\Big/ p_{t+1}$$

or

$$p_{t+1} = \frac{e_y}{e_z} \cdot p_t - \frac{2m_t}{e_z}. \tag{1}$$

The stationary solution to this difference equation is given by

$$p_{t+1} = p_t = p^s = \frac{2m_t}{e_y/e_z}. \tag{2}$$

This is the stationary competitive equilibrium price system. Difference equation (1) has other solutions with positive prices. As $e_y/e_z > 1$ by assumption, given any $p_o \geq p^s$, the price sequence generated by (1) is a competitive equilibrium price system. Note that except for $p_o = p^s$, the equilibrium price sequence increases geometrically towards infinity. This implies asymptotically that individuals will just consume their endowment as money becomes worthless.

Design of Experiments

Four laboratory economies, numbered chronologically for reference in this paper, were conducted, Economies 1 and 2 involved double oral auctions.[4] In Economies 3 and 4, market clearing price and allocations each period were computed from the supply functions solicited from the members of the "young"

[4] A double oral auction is conducted as follows: Any seller (buyer) is free to state a price at which he/she is willing to sell (buy) one chip. Any other seller (buyer) can offer to sell (buy) at a lower (higher) price than the current offer (bid). Any buyer (seller) can accept the current offer (bid). When an acceptance is made, the respective traders enter into a binding contract to buy-sell one chip.

generation.[5] We describe the design of Economy 1 before outlining how the three subsequent economies differed from the first. Instructions for Economies 3 and 4 are given in the Appendix. Other instructions are available from the authors on request.

Economy 1 had 14 subjects of which four were randomly picked each period to form a generation. Each generation lived for two periods labelled entry and exit periods respectively. Thus during any given period, eight subjects were active participants in the economy while six sat idle. The next generation was formed by random selection from these six subjects. This procedure ensured that each subject sat idle for at least one period after exiting the game and before reentering it. The entry and exit plan in the Appendix shows the sequence of participation by individual subjects.

Each subject was endowed with seven chips at the beginning of the entry period and one chip at the beginning of the exit period. The entry period endowment of money (called francs in the experiment) was zero. Any money received from the sale of chips during the entry period was carried over by each subject to the exit period when it could be used to buy chips. Each subject for whom the first period itself was the exit period was given 1000 francs. No further money was injected into the economy.

Subjects were allowed a period of five minutes to engage in a double oral auction for purchase and sale of chips for francs. Entry subjects could only sell while exit subjects could only buy chips. The number of chips on hand with each subject was not allowed to go below one and the balance of francs was not allowed to go below zero during trading. If a buyer had insufficient cash to buy a whole chip at the prevailing price, he or she had the option to buy an appropriate fraction to use up the cash balance. Any francs left in the hands of the exit subjects at the end of the five-minute trading period were permanently lost from the economy.

At the end of trading during the exit period, traders of that generation calculated their "winning number" by multiplying the number of chips held at the end of entry period (y_t) and at the end of the exit period z_{t+1}. They received a fixed reward of \$6.00 with probability proportional to the log of the "winning number" as follows:

$$\text{Prob. (reward} = \$6) = \log (y_t \cdot z_{t+1})/\log(30).$$

[5] These auctions were conducted as follows. Each seller (member of the young generation) was asked to offer a schedule of prices at which he/she was willing to sell up to 0, 1, 2, ..., 7 chips. Individual supply function was created by linear interpolation between discreet points specified by the seller. The market supply function was the sum of individual supply functions. All money in the hands of the buyers (members of the old generation in this experiment) was used to construct a hyperbolic (fixed revenue) demand function. Market clearing price and quantities were determined at the intersection of the supply and demand functions. The market clearing price and quantity were announced and each trader was informed individually about the number of chips bought or sold by him or her.

A prize wheel with log scale markings was used to determine if the subject received a $6 or zero reward.[6] Subjects were given training to familiarize them with the probabilistic mechanism.

The subjects knew in advance that the game would last for approximately three hours. They were also informed that at the end of the game, francs in the hands of the subjects would be converted into chips at the mean transaction price of the last period actually played. The transaction price data was recorded on a blackboard during each period and a running summary of trading each period (number of transactions, opening, closing, highest, lowest and mean prices) was maintained in full view of the subjects on the blackboard.

Design of Economy 2 was similar to Economy 1 except that the francs given to "old" subjects in the first period were reduced to 250 from 1000 to change the initial stationary competitive equilibrium price from 333 to 83 francs. Nine of the subjects who participated in Economy 1 participated in Economy 2. Five new subjects were recruited for the study.

Economies 3 and 4 were designed as supply schedule auctions with some other innovations. First, we wished to test the robustness of the stationary equilibrium to a variety of auction mechanisms. Second, double oral auction required five minutes of hectic trading. Between trading and keeping their accounts, it was argued, the subjects had little time for reflection and to think about the future and to try to anticipate what might happen during the next period. Supply schedule auction simplifies the task of the subjects. It assigns a passive role to the buyers in our experiment. The role of sellers was limited to preparing a supply schedule specified at eight discreet points. This environment presumably places less severe demands on the cognitive resources of the subjects and thus permits more time for reflection. Third, it was difficult to prevent money from being permanently lost to the market in the double oral auctions because the exit subjects did not always use up all their cash balance to buy chips, due to accounting errors, misunderstanding or lack of time. The effect was a changing value of the price predicted by stationary competitive equilibrium. Five-minute trading time followed by accounting calculations allowed only about six periods to be run each hour which limited the total number of replications that could be carried out within the limited time available. Finally, in the heat of hectic trading, subjects made accounting errors that also resulted in either random loss or injection of money to the economy. Most of these problems could easily be handled through a supply schedule auction with the assistance of a personal computer and an appropriate monitoring program.

Two more changes were made between the first and the last two economies. The probabilistic reward mechanism was replaced by a deterministic one with rewards proportional to $(y_t \cdot z_{t+1})^{1/2}$. Also, at the beginning of each period, the nonparticipating subjects were asked to make a prediction of the market clear-

[6] The purpose of using the prize wheel and probabilistic reward scheme was to induce the subjects to be risk averse in consumption during each period. See Berg et al. (1986).

Table 1. Steps of experimental procedure

Economies 1 and 2

1. Training (two periods of transaction examples and prize wheel).
2. Experimenter announces entry subjects.
3. Double oral auction between entry and exit subjects.
4. Experimenter announces the end of the period.
5. Participating subjects calculate ending balances of chips and money.
6. Exit subjects spin prize wheels and record their profit.
7. Go to step 2.

Economies 3 and 4

1. Training (two periods of transaction examples).
2. Experimenter announces entry subjects.
3. Non-participating subjects record market price prediction.
4. Experimenter collects prediction sheets, and keys predictions into the computer.
5. Entry subjects record supply schedules on offer sheets.
6. Experimenter collects offer sheets and enters them into the computer.
7. Experimenter announces market clearing price, trading volume, average prediction, and the winner of the price prediction contest, and distributes individual allocations.
8. All subjects record market outcome and exit subjects record their profit.
9. Go to step 2.

ing price of the period. After the market clearing price was announced, the subject with the closest prediction was given a reward of $2.00. Subjects were also informed that at the end of the game (approximately three hours from the start) money balances in the hands of the subjects would be converted into chips at the exchange rate determined by the average prediction made for that period. Thus in all economies, the price of "chips" at the end of the game was determined endogenously and not dictated by the experimenter. Moreover, the procedure for ending the game was clearly explained to the subjects at the outset.

Subjects were undergraduate business majors at the University of Minnesota. Nine out of fourteen subjects who participated in Economy 1 also participated in Economy 2. Five new subjects in Economy 2 were given instruction before participating. Fourteen new subjects were recruited for Economy 3, of which eight also participated in Economy 4. Three subjects from Economies 1 and 2 participated in Economy 4. Since only 11 subjects could attend Economy 4, each generation consisted of three instead of four subjects.

The sequence of main steps in the economies is given in Table 1 and the key design features of the four economies are given in Table 2.

Table 2. Design of experiments

Expt. No.	Market Type	Location	Experience	Number of Subjects in the Experiment /in each Generation	Chip Endowment		Money Endowment* (francs)		(Expected) Payoff Function	Prize Wheel
					Entry	Exit	Entry	Exit		
1	Double Oral	U. of Minnesota	Inexperienced	14/4	7	1	1,000	0	$\$6\,\frac{\log(y_t \cdot z_{t+1})}{\log 30}$	Yes
2	Double Oral	"	Experienced (9/14)	14/4	7	1	250	0	$\$6\,\frac{\log(y_t \cdot z_{t+1})}{\log 30}$	Yes
3	Supply Schedule	"	Inexperienced	14/4	7	1	1,000	0	$\$1.20(y_t \cdot z_{t+1})^{1/2}$	No
4	Supply Schedule	"	Experienced	11/3	7	1	250	0	$\$0.75(y_t \cdot z_{t+1})^{1/2}$	No

* Money endowment was given only in the first period. No further money was injected into the economy.

Equilibrium Predictions

Two kinds of ideas can be applied to calculate the price and allocations predicted under a stationary equilibrium. In a competitive equilibrium where each trader acts as a price taker, the stationary equilibrium price is given by

$$p = 2m/(e_y - e_z)$$

where m is the amount of money per person, e_y is the chip endowment per subject in the entry period and e_z is the chip endowment per subject in the exit period. Under this equilibrium, each entry period subject will sell $(e_y - e_z)/2$ chips and each exit subject will buy the same number of chips and therefore hold $(e_y + e_z)/2$ chips at the end of each period. This equilibrium maximizes the payoff from the experimenter to the subjects. Parameters of the four economies, and the price, allocation, and (expected) profit predictions of the stationary competitive equilibrium model are given in the first few columns of Table 3.

While price-taking behavior may be a reasonable approximation when the number of traders is large, one may reasonably question if the predictions of the competitive model can describe the data well when the number of buyers and sellers is three or four each. Predictions of stationary Nash equilibrium can be derived under the assumption that traders choose their supply functions optimally, relative to their assumption about the behavior of the others and such assumptions are consistent with their own behavior. There is a continuum of symmetric stationary Nash equilibria of which stationary competitive equilibrium allocation represents one extreme case.

Suppose individual i sells s_i units in youth and expects to buy goods at price p^f in old age. Since the total amount of money in the economy is $m \cdot n$ units, individual i enters old age with cash $m \cdot n \cdot s_i \Big/ \left(\sum_{j=1}^{n} s_j \right)$ that can be used to buy $m \cdot n \cdot s_i \Big/ \left(p^f \cdot \sum_{j=1}^{n} s_j \right)$ units of good in old age. Therefore, i's maximization problem can be written as

$$\max_{s_i} (e_y - s_i)\left(e_z + m \cdot n \cdot s_i \Big/ \left(p^f \cdot \sum_{j=1}^{n} s_j \right) \right) .$$

The first order condition evaluated at $s_i = s$ is

$$m\left(\frac{n-1}{n}\right)\left(\frac{e_y - s}{p^f \cdot s}\right) = e_z + \frac{m}{p^f} .$$

Setting $p^f = p = m/s$ yields the extreme symmetric stationary Nash solution:

$$p^N = \frac{m(2n-1)}{(n-1)e_y - ne_z} , \tag{3}$$

which is greater than or equal to the stationary competitive price p^s given in the equation (2). The range of symmetric stationary Nash equilibria is p^N to p^s. This

Table 3. Equilibrium predictions

Expt. No.	Competitive Equilibrium			Extreme Nash Equilibrium			Demonetized Economy		
	Price	Number of chips Traded*	Profit[a] per person per 2-period life	Price	Number of chips Traded*	(Expected) Profit[a] per person per 2-period life	Price	Number of chips Traded	(Expected) Profit[a] of chips per 2-period life
1	333	3	$4.89	412	2.43	$4.85		0	$3.43
2	83	3	$4.89	103	2.43	$4.85		0	$3.43
3	333	3	$4.80	412	2.43	$4.75		0	$3.17
4	83	3	$3.00	114	2.19	$2.94		0	$1.98

* Per capita
[a] Profit for each Entry-Exit pair

range is marked on Figures 1 through 4. As $n \to \infty$, $p^N \to p^s$ and the range converges to zero. Since we used $n = 4$ and 3, p^N/p^s is 21/17 and 15/11 respectively. The price, allocation and profit predictions of the stationary Nash equilibrium of each of the four economies are given in Table 3.

From the continuum of nonstationary equilibria, it is worth mentioning at least one extreme case of a demonetized economy in which the price of chips in terms of money increases without bound and the money becomes worthless. In this equilibrium, all subjects stay with their endowment of chips and receive a relatively low level of payoff from the experimenter. The predictions of this model are also given in Table 3.

Results

Price

Figures 1 and 2 show the prices of individual transactions during each period of Economies 1 and 2 respectively. Figure 3 and 4 show the market clearing prices for each period of Economies 3 and 4 respectively. Stationary competitive equilibrium price is shown by a horizontal line at the lower edge of the hatched area in all figures. The horizontal line at the upper edge of the hatched area marks the upper extreme stationary Nash equilibrium price. Downward shifts in equilibrium prices in Economies 1 and 2 were caused mostly by loss of money in the economy due to the inability of the old generation to utilize all the money they had to purchase "chips." The loss of money to the economy was permanent, and was not recouped through redistribution. Most of this shift occurred in the early periods of each experiment. All the upward shifts in the equilibrium price and some downward shifts occurred due to accounting mistakes by subjects, and they remained undiscovered until the data sheets were tabulated and analyzed by the experimenters. Thus, stationary equilibrium in Economies 1 and 2 in fact constituted a moving, though well-defined, target over the periods. The switch to supply schedule auction in Economies 3 and 4 was motivated in part by our desire to test the market behavior under conditions where stationary equilibrium remained unchanged from period to period. The changing equilibrium price did, as we argue later in this section, allow us to test the robustness of the stationary equilibrium concept under conditions of "stochastically" changing money supply.

In all four economies, the price of "chips" in terms of francs is substantially different from the competitive stationary equilibrium (CSE) in the first period. In the first period of Economies 1 and 2, the average transaction price is 60

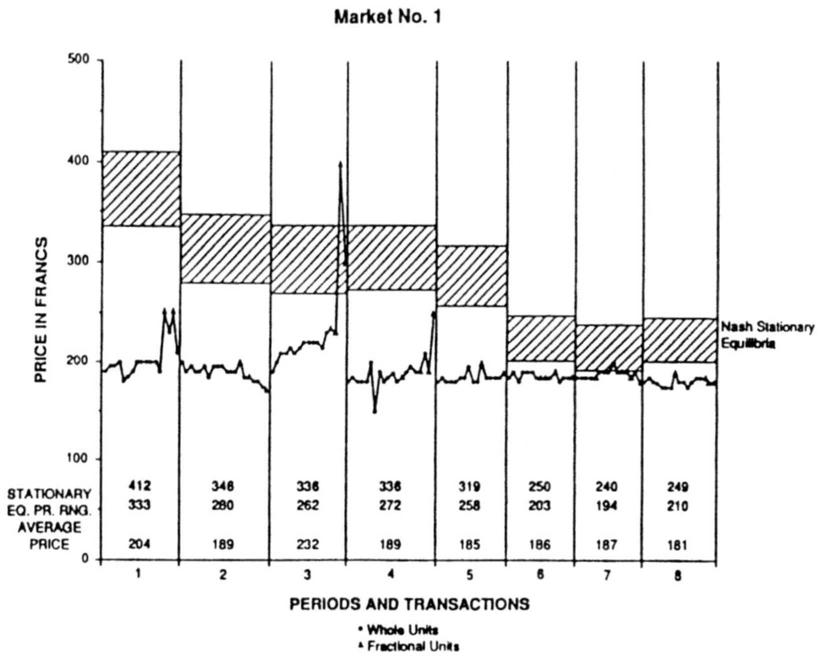

Fig. 1. Transaction prices

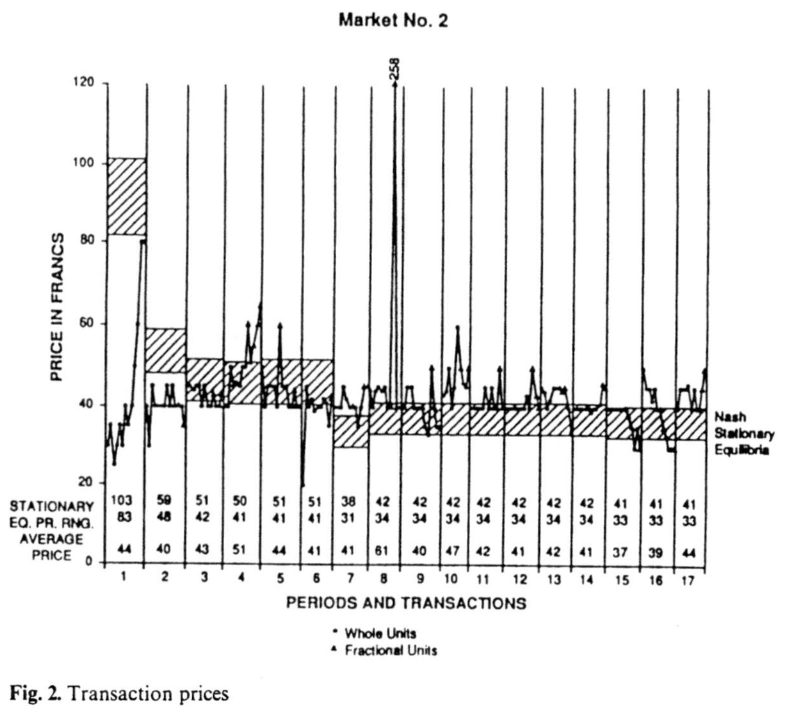

Fig. 2. Transaction prices

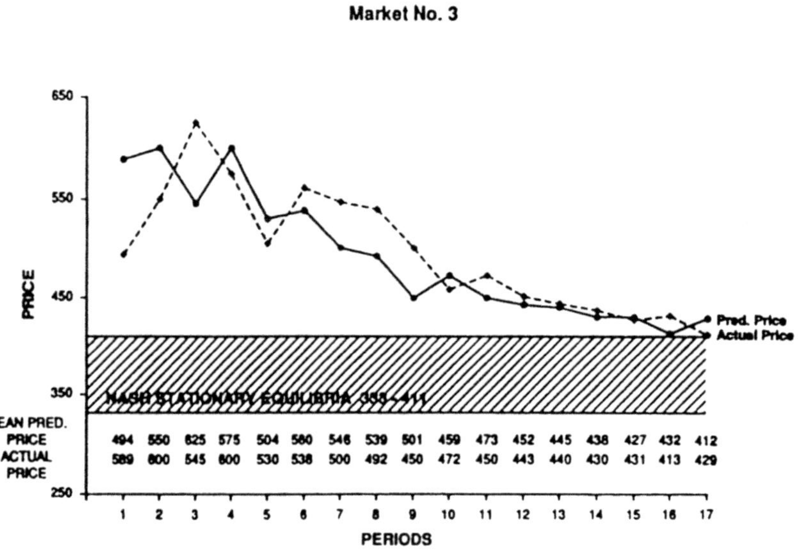

Fig. 3. Transaction prices

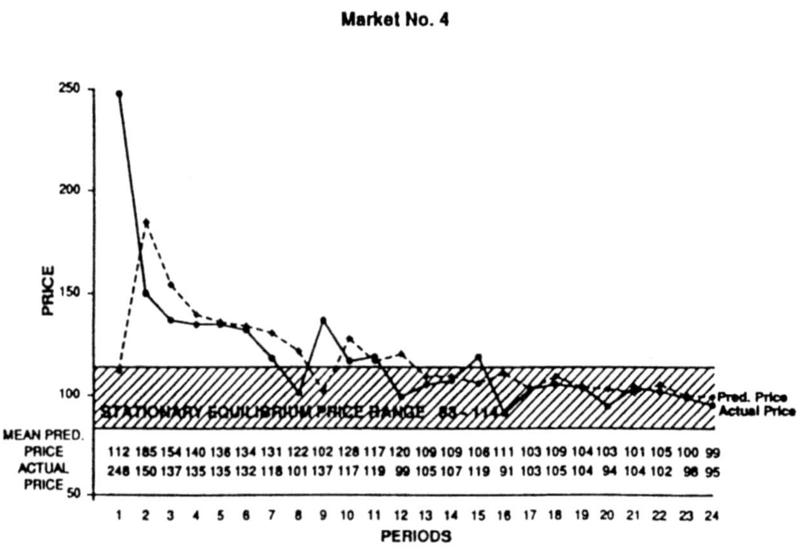

Fig. 4. Transaction prices

percent and 53 percent respectively of the CSE price. This percentage changes to 90 and 125 in the last period of the respective economies. In Economy 1, the change is more or less monotonic. In Economy 2, most of the change occurs in the first and second periods; and price is almost randomly distributed about 40 thereafter. In Economy 3, the market clearing price declines from 176 percent of CSE price in the first period to 129 percent in the last period. In Economy 4 the market clearing price declines from 300 percent of CSE to 112 percent. With replication there is a marked convergence towards stationary equilibrium though the convergence is not precise. To what extent further replications may affect the nature of convergence is an open question.

It is possible to interpret the evidence on price in support of the stationary equilibrium. Besides the observation of price in the neighborhood of the stationary equilibria, perhaps an even more striking aspect of the data is the rather stable nature of the price path. Even if the data cannot be said to support the stationary equilibrium, in no case can it be said to be consistent with demonetization of the economy. In both double oral auctions (Economies 1 and 2), some transactions occurred at very high prices and they could have provided a basis for the markets to take a path of exponential growth in prices. However, such high-price transactions seem not to have been followed by other high-price transactions and the markets continued on relatively stable paths.

As we discussed earlier, the loss of unutilized money in the hands of the old generation in Economies 1 and 2 amounted to a random demand shock to the economy in each period. The shock was random because none of the participants in the market that suffered such a demand shock knew about the fact of the extent of the loss of money in the economy. Recall that after exiting the game, each subject waited on the sidelines for at least one period before reentering. This random demand shock was another reason for the economy not to converge to the stationary equilibrium. The fact that the economy still seemed to converge in the neighborhood of the CSE is, to our eyes, evidence in the support of the robustness of the stationary equilibrium.

Volume

In Economies 3 and 4, volume is inversely proportional to the price of "chips" and therefore all information contained in volume is contained in the price variable. In all economies, CSE trading volume was 3 "chips" per capita and the extreme Nash Stationary Equilibrium (NSE) trading volume was 2.43 "chips" per person in Economies 1, 2 and 3, and 2.19 in Economy 4. In a demonetized economy, trading volume would be zero. The actual trading volume relative to these benchmarks is shown in the four panels of Figure 5. These results support the inference drawn in support of the stationary equilibrium.

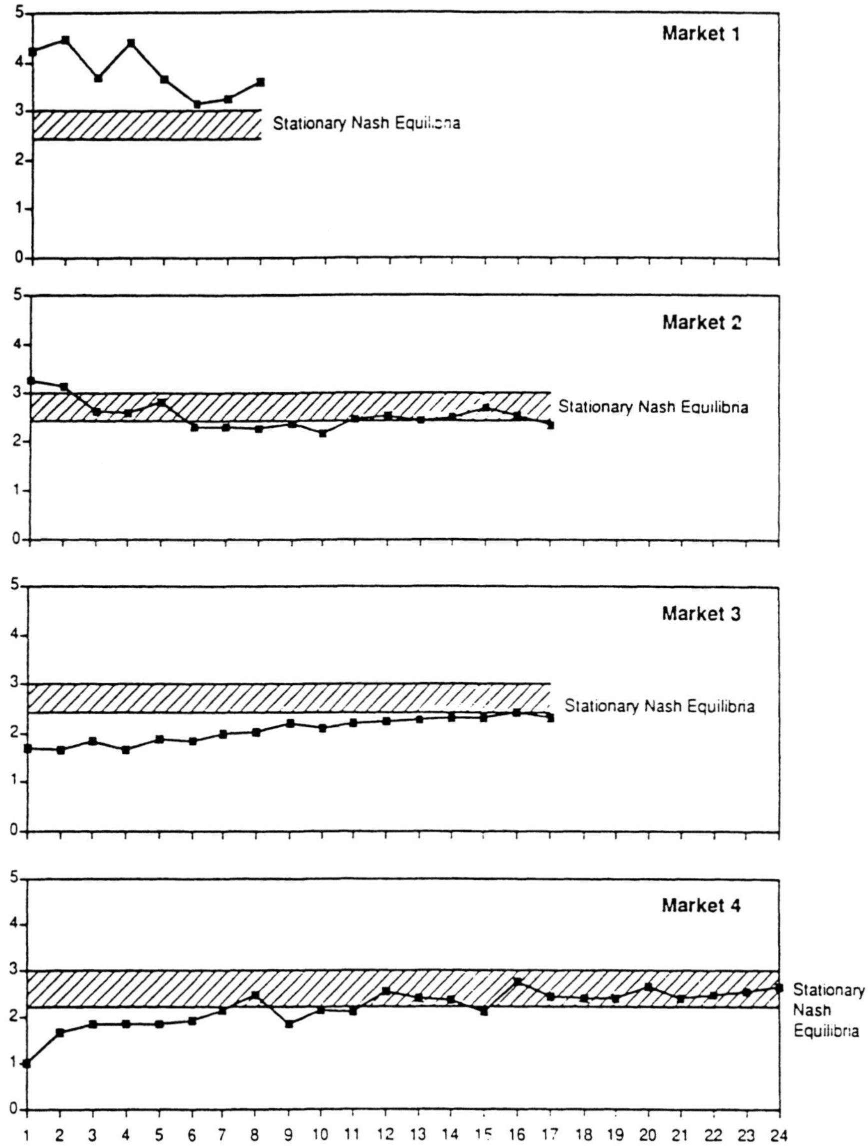

Fig. 5. Per capita trading volume

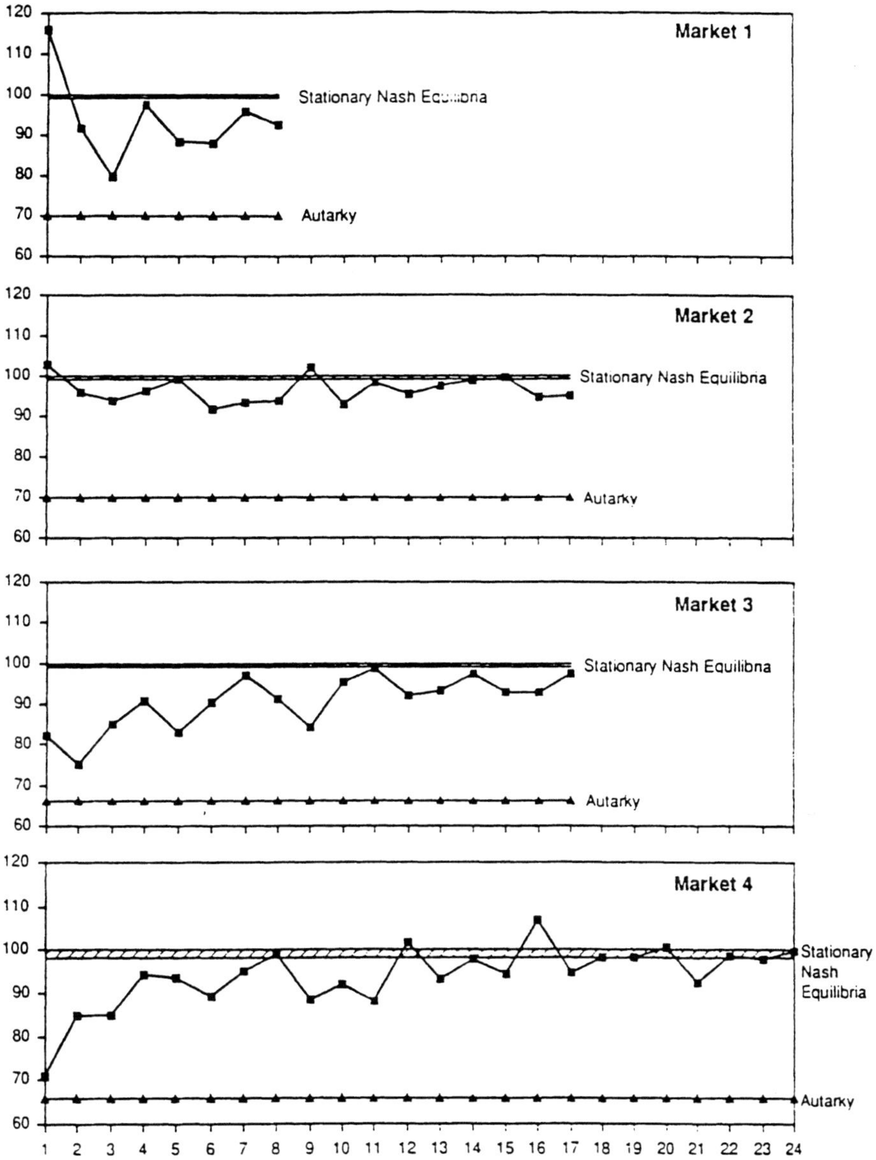

Fig. 6. Efficiency of markets

Efficiency

In Economies 1 and 2 which have probabilistic payoffs, we use the expected dollar payoff achieved by the exit subjects each period as a percentage of the maximum possible expected payoff achievable, as the measure of efficiency. In Economies 3 and 4 where the payoff is deterministic, efficiency is measured by the actual dollar payoff received by the exit subjects as a percentage of the maximum possible dollar payoff. The efficiency of all four markets is shown in Figure 6. The maximum payoff is attained for CSE and the 100 percent efficiency line corresponds to this equilibrium. A demonetized economy has no trades, and the efficiency corresponding to the endowment distribution of "chips" is the lower benchmark (autarky) in the efficiency charts.

All four markets can be seen to be highly efficient with the efficiency reaching as high as 98 percent. The average efficiency of Economies 1, 2, 3 and 4 is 93.7%, 96.5%, 90.5%, and 93.9% respectively. Compared to the 66–70 percent bench mark for demonetized economies, these data leave little doubt that the stationary equilibrium is a reasonable candidate to explain the behavior of these economies.

Concluding Remarks

The substantive finding of our experiment is that the stationary solutions to the overlapping generations model of fiat money form the domain of attraction for the behavior of these experimental economies. Since the initial price in all experimental economies deviated significantly from the stationary solutions, there was every chance for these economies to follow nonstationary paths. The fact that all these economies stabilized close to the range of stationary solutions suggests that stationary solutions are better descriptors of behavior in such environments. Further, our conclusions are robust relative to two different institutions for organizing exchange transactions.

With the exception of Economy 1, all economies converged towards the upper end of the range of stationary Nash solutions as opposed to the lower end defined by the competitive stationary solution. The data therefore suggest that the young did exploit some of their monopsony power. Experiments with more subjects would reduce this power.

In Economies 3 and 4, as subjects gained experience, and as the economy stabilized close to the stationary equilibrium, the quality of forecasts improved. Forecasts appear to be adaptive though we have not carried out a formal analysis.

Finally, we experimented with two different techniques of bringing laboratory experiments of indefinitely lived economies to an end. Converting end-of-the-game money balances into goods at (1) price observed in the last period and at (2) price forecast made during the last period, seem to be satisfactorily neutral devices for terminating such economies.

Appendix

Instructions and Experimental Procedures

In Economies 1 and 2, markets were conducted in three steps: (1) training for the payoff mechanism with prize wheels; (2) training with two periods of sample transactions; and (3) main markets. At the beginning, subjects were randomly assigned their subject numbers and seated on prearranged seats with tables. On each table, a packet of instructions and forms was placed in advance. Subjects were not allowed to talk to one another.

Step 1: First instruction set (not included here) was read aloud. All subjects were asked to decide the number of chips to be purchased and then were asked to spin a prize wheel. The profit (prize won minus the cost of chips bought) was paid. This process was repeated about 10 to 15 times.

Step 2: Second instruction set (not included here) was read aloud. Two trial periods were conducted. In the first period, half the subjects played entry-period players and the other half exit-period players. In the second period, the roles were reversed to give all the subjects equal experience. Chip endowment for entry-period subjects was four chips and money endowment for initial exit-period subjects was 10,000 francs. All other parameters were the same as shown in Table 1. A set of transaction examples was shown on the projection screen. Subjects were asked to speak out their respective bids and offers in the examples shown. At the end of each period, they were asked to spin Prize Wheel 2. Individual record sheets were checked for possible errors.

Step 3: Actual overlapping generations economy was conducted. At the beginning of each five-minute period, the experimenter asked for bids and offers. A "one minute left" warning was issued before the market ended. At the end of each period, the experimenter checked the accuracy of record sheets and watched subjects spin prize wheels.

In Economies 3 and 4, markets were conducted in two steps: (1) training with two periods of example transactions; (2) actual experiment.

Step 1: The instruction set (see the following pages) was read aloud and explained. Transaction examples were shown on the screen. Half the subjects played entry subjects and the others exit subjects in the first example period, and the roles were reversed in the second. Subjects were asked to fill in their individual record sheets, including price prediction sheets, so each subject would understand how the market was to proceed and his/her profit would be calculated. The experimenter distributed pre-processed individual computer outputs. All the subjects were asked to record the market outcome from the computer outputs. The same process was repeated in the second period.

Step 2: Main markets were preceded by the procedure explained in the Design of Experiments section. At the beginning of each period, the experimenter showed entry and exit subjects of the period on the screen and asked the subjects not participating in that period to submit market price predictions and the entry subjects to submit their supply schedules. Supply schedules were entered into the computer and the experimenter announced the resultant market clearing price, the market clearing quantity, the average prediction price and the winner of the price prediction contest on the blackboard. Then the experimenter distributed computer-printed slips of paper indicating price and quantity bought/sold by them to the subjects and to the winner of the prediction contest. This process was repeated each period.

Instructions

This is an experiment in decision-making. Various research foundations have provided funds for this research. The instructions are simple, and if you follow them carefully and make good decisions, you might earn a considerable amount of money which will be paid to you in cash.

In this experiment, we are going to have a market in which you will buy and sell chips in a sequence of market periods. Attached to these instructions you will find sheets labelled Information and Record Sheet, Selling Offer Sheet and Market Price Prediction Sheet which help you record your decisions and determine their value to you.

The type of currency used in this market is francs. The only use of this currency is to buy and sell chips. It has no other use. The money you take home with you is in dollars. The procedures for determining the number of dollars you take home with you is explained later in these instructions.

You will participate in the market for two consecutive periods at a time. Let us call the first of these periods *your* entry period (because you begin your participation then) and the second of these periods *your* exit period (because you end your participation in the market). Different individuals may have different entry and exit periods and the experimenter will inform you about when you will enter and exit the market. You may be asked to enter and exit more than once depending on the number of periods for which the market is operated.

At the beginning of your entry period, you will receive 7 chips from the experimenter and at the beginning of your exit period you will receive 1 chip. In your entry period, you may keep these chips or sell chips to others. In your exit period, you can buy more chips from others but you cannot sell. Buying and selling of chips will occur in francs according to the rules to be explained later.

The product of the number of chips you hold at the end of trading each period determines the amount of money you earn for that pair of entry-exit periods. The experimenter will calculate the square root of the product and multiply it by $1.20 to calculate the amount of dollars you earn. Thus, suppose you hold 5 chips at the end of your entry period and 3.5 chips at the end of your exit period. The product of these two numbers is $5 \times 3.5 = 17.5$. The square root of 17.5 is 4.18 which is multiplied by $1.20 to yield $5.02 as your earning in these two periods. Note that the higher the product of the numbers of chips held by you at the end of entry and exit periods, the higher is the profit you earn. Also note that if you hold zero chips at the end of either period, your profits will be zero because the product of zero with any other finite number is zero. All chips are returned to the experimenter at the end of each period.

The first period of the market will be an entry period for some of you (as described above). For some of you, however, this first period itself will be an exit period and you will receive the exit period endowment of 1 chip at the beginning of this period. In addition, each of you for whom the first period is an exit period will receive 1,000 francs from the experimenter at the beginning of this period. You have to use all these francs to buy chips during the exit period because the francs you hold at the end of an exit period are worthless; they cannot be converted into dollars directly.

When you sell chips, your holding of chips decreases and your holding of francs increases by the amount of the price of the chips. Similarly, when you buy chips, your holding of chips increases and your holding of francs vanishes.

At the end of each period, all your chips on hand are used up to earn profits in dollars and thus returned to the experimenter. The francs you have on hand at the end of the entry period are carried over to the exit period and used to buy chips in this latter period.

All outside-market players participate in the market indirectly. At the beginning of each period, each outsider-market player predicts the market price of the period. The average of the predicted price will be used to convert the francs held by the entry-period players to chips at the end of the experiment. A $2.00 prize will be given to the player whose prediction is the closest to the actual market price. If there is a tie, the prize will be split.

Trading and Recording Rules

1) All entry-period players are sellers and all exit-period players are buyers.
2) Every exit-period player must pay all his francs to entry-period players in exchange for chips at a *market price* determined below.
3) At the beginning of each period, every entry-period player must state the following prices on the Selling Offer Sheet and submit it to the experimenter. If the prices you submit are not nondecreasing in the number of chips offered, we shall make them so.

   Price below which you don't want to sell any chips —— francs/chip;
   Price at which you are willing to sell up to 1 chip —— francs/chip;
   Price at which you are willing to sell up to 2 chips —— francs/chip;
   Price at which you are willing to sell up to 3 chips —— francs/chip;
   Price at which you are willing to sell up to 4 chips —— francs/chip;
   Price at which you arc willing to sell up to 5 chips —— francs/chip;
   Price at which you are willing to sell up to 6 chips —— francs/chip;
   Price at which you are willing to sell up to 7 chips —— francs/chip;

4) The experimenter collects the Selling Offer Sheets from all entry period players, and after considering the amount of francs available from the exit-period players, computes and announces the market clearing price. Each entry-period player will be informed of the number of chips he/she has been able to sell at the market price, and each exit-period player will be told of the number of chips that he/she has been able to buy with his/her francs on hand.

   Note that if you (entry-period player) do not specify a price for zero chip, up to one chip of yours may be sold at zero francs. If you do not want to sell more than a specified number of chips under any circumstances, specify a very high price. This is the only way you have of not wanting to sell. The actual number of chips you sell will almost always be in fractions, depending on the market clearing price. The way the market clearing mechanism works, if you are willing to sell, say two units at unit price x and 3 units at unit price y, you may end up selling, say 2.4 units at a price between x and y.
5) At the beginning of each period, each outside-market player writes down a predicted market price on the Market Price Prediction Sheet which is collected by the experimenter. At the end of each period, the experimenter announces average predicted market price and the winner(s) – the outside-market players whose prediction was the closest to the actual market price. This player records *$2.00* prize on the Market Price Prediction Sheet. But, when there is more than one winner, the prize is split. All other outside-market players record *$0* prize on the sheet.
6) After the transaction information is received from the experimenter, each

entry-period player computes the chips remaining on hand and the francs received from sale and records them on the Information and Record Sheet.

7) Each exit-period player records the number of chips purchased on the Information and Record Sheet. Then the experimenter computes the product of the number of chips held by each exit-period player at the end of entry and exit periods respectively, takes the square root of the product and multiplies by *$1.20*. This amount is the profit of the exit-period player who records this profit on the Information and Record Sheet. At the conclusion of the experiment, the experimenter will pay each player the total amount of profits made.
8) The francs received by the entry-period players in the entry period will be used to buy chips in the exit period which follows immediately. So, carry your francs on hand forward to the exit period by entering them in the column Beginning-Francs on Hand on the Information and Record Sheet.
9) At the end of the experiment, francs held by *all entry-period* players are converted into chips using the average of predicted market prices by outside-market players.
10) At the end of the experiment, add up the profit column of your Information and Record Sheet. The experimenter will pay you this amount of money.

Entry and Exit Plan for Economy 1

(N = entry, X = exit)

	Subject Number													(14 Subjects)
Period	*1*	*2*	*3*	*4*	*5*	*6*	*7*	*8*	*9*	*10*	*11*	*12*	*13*	*14*
1	N	–	X	–	N	X	N	–	X	X	–	N	–	–
2	X	N	–	–	X	–	X	N	–	–	N	X	N	–
3	–	X	–	N	–	N	–	X	N	–	X	–	X	N
4	N	–	N	X	–	X	N	–	X	N	–	–	–	X
5	X	N	X	–	N	–	X	N	–	X	–	N	–	–
6	–	X	–	N	X	–	–	X	–	–	N	X	N	N
7	–	–	N	X	–	N	–	–	N	N	X	–	X	X
8	N	N	X	–	–	X	N	N	X	X	–	–	–	–
9	X	X	–	N	N	–	X	X	–	–	N	–	N	–
10	–	–	N	X	X	–	–	–	–	N	X	N	X	N
11	–	N	X	–	–	N	–	N	N	X	–	X	–	X
12	N	X	–	–	N	X	N	X	X	–	N	–	–	–
13	X	–	–	N	X	–	X	–	–	–	X	N	N	N
14	–	N	N	X	–	N	–	–	–	N	–	X	X	X
15	–	X	X	–	N	X	N	–	N	X	N	–	–	–
16	N	–	–	N	X	–	X	N	X	–	X	N	–	–
17	X	N	N	X	–	–	–	X	–	N	–	X	N	–
18	–	X	X	–	N	–	–	–	N	X	N	–	X	N
19	N	–	–	–	X	–	N	N	X	–	X	N	–	X
20	X	N	N	–	–	N	X	X	–	N	–	X	–	–

Training Sheets

Player No. __________

Period No.	Entry / Exit	Beginning Francs on Hand	Beginning Chips on Hand	Chips Sold	Chips Purchased	Ending Francs on Hand	Ending Chips on Hand	Profit ($)
	Entry	0	5					
	Exit		1			0		
	Entry	0	5					
	Exit		1			0		
	Entry	0	5					
	Exit		1			0		

Period No.	Unit Selling-Offer Prices (francs) for: 0 Chip	1 Chip	2 Chips	3 Chips	4 Chips	5 Chips	6 Chips	7 Chips	Market Price	Chips Sold

Period No.	Predicted Market Price (francs)	Actual Market Price (francs)	Prize ($)

References

Azariadis C (1982) Self fulfilling prophecies. Journal of Economic Theory 25:380–396.

Berg J, Daley L, Dickhaut J, O'Brien J (1986) Controlling preferences for units of experimental exchange. Quarterly Journal of Economics 101:2, 201–306

Calvo G (1978) On the indeterminacy of interest rates and wages with perfect foresight. Journal of Economic Theory 19:321–37

Cass D, Shell C (1983) Do sunspots matter? Journal of Political Economy 91:2, 193–227

Grandmont J (1986) Stabilizing competitive business cycles. Journal of Economic Theory 40:1, 57–76

Kehoe TJ, Levine DK (1985) Comparative statics and perfect foresight in infinite horizon models. Econometrica 53:433–453

Lucas RE Jr (1972). Expectations and the neutrality of money. Journal of Economic Theory 4:103–24

Lucas RE Jr (1986) Adaptive behavior and economic theory. Journal of Business 59:S401–S426

Marimon R, Spear SE, Sunder S (1993) Expectationally-driven market volatility: Experimental evidence. Journal of Economic Theory 61:1, 74–103

Marimon R, Sunder S (1993) Indeterminacy of equilibria in a hyperinflationary world: Experimental evidence. Econometrica 61:1073–1107

Marimon R, Sunder S. (1994) Expectations and learning under alternative monetary regimes: An experimental approach. Economic Theory 4:131–162

Samuelson PA (1958) An exact consumption-loan model of interest with or without the social contrivance of money. Journal of Political Economy 66:467–82

Shubik M (1973) Commodity money, oligopoly, credit and bankruptcy in a general equilibrium model. Western Economic Journal 11:1, 24–38

Spear S, Srivastava S (1985) Indeterminacy and sun spots in a stochastic overlapping generations model. Carnegie Mellon Working Paper

Wallace N (1980) The overlapping generations model of fiat money. In: Kareken JH, Wallace N (Eds.) Models of Monetary Economics. Minneapolis, Federal Reserve Bank of Minneapolis. 49–82

Lets Keep the Con out of Experimental Econ.: A Methodological Note

ALVIN E. ROTH

Department of Economics, Faculty of Arts and Sciences, University of Pittsburgh, Pittsburgh PA 15260, USA

JEL-Classification System-Numbers: C90, C91, C92

When Edward Leamer (1983) wrote the well known critique of econometric practice whose title I have adapted and adopted, he was concerned that the credibility and utility of econometric research had suffered because of differences between the way econometric research was conducted and the way it was reported[1]. He wrote (p36–37):

"The econometric art as it is practiced at the computer terminal involves fitting many, perhaps thousands, of statistical models. One or several that the researcher finds pleasing are selected for reporting purposes. This searching for a model is often well intentioned, but there can be no doubt that such a specification search invalidates the traditional theories of inference. The concepts of unbiasedness, consistency, efficiency, maximum-likelihood estimation, in fact, all the concepts of traditional theory, utterly lose their meaning by the time an applied researcher pulls from the bramble of computer output the one thorn of a model he likes best, the one he chooses to portray as a rose. The consuming public is hardly fooled by this chicanery."

Leamer emphasized the contrast between the problems facing an econometrician and those facing an experimenter. He used agricultural experiments as his example of experimental research, and suggested that experimental methods, both in the laboratory and in the field, might prove increasingly useful to economists.

In the intervening years, the rapid growth of laboratory experiments in economics has amply justified this confidence. While we still have much to learn about the uses of experimentation in economics, it is already clear that carefully controlled experiments permit us to draw some kinds of inferences with far more confidence than we could hope to do from any available nonexperimental data.

At the same time, experimental economists, like econometricians, need to be careful not to let the way we report experiments diverge in important dimensions from the way they are sometimes actually conducted. This has become increasingly clear in the last ten years, as there have begun to be enough experi-

---

[1] See also the earlier related critique by Feige [1975], who focused on the incentives for questionable reporting practices inadvertently encouraged by the editorial policies of professional journals, a point to which I shall return in the conclusion. Both Feige and Leamer refrained from citing by name any particularly egregious examples in the literature of the practices they criticized. I will follow their example, in order not to transform into personal criticism what I intend to be remarks of potential relevance to all experimenters.

mental economists so that it is no longer unusual for experimenters with different theoretical predispositions to be investigating the same questions. Some thought is in order about how to report experiments so as to make these dialogues as efficient and informative as possible. In this regard, there are useful things to be learned from the older experimental traditions in other sciences. This is so even though, as we gain more experience with economic experiments, we see that they do not look exactly like experiments in agriculture, or chemistry, or medicine, or even in psychology, but rather that the nascent tradition of experimental economics has some distinguishing characteristics. And indeed, some of the issues we need to pay attention to, to make sure that we report economic experiments in a way that is as informative as possible about the way we conduct them, arise from these distinctive features of economic experimentation.

My purpose here is to raise some of these issues, concerning how and in what detail we report experimental procedures, what data is reported, how it is aggregated for reporting purposes, and how it is analyzed. Some of the potential pitfalls facing experimenters are similar to those facing econometricians: when pilot experiments are used to search through alternative experimental procedures and parameters, and to decide which experimental investigations shall proceed to the reporting stage, then, if this is not fully reported, it is easy to misinterpret the significance and robustness of the reported results.

Many of these issues can be highlighted by focusing on a deceptively simple matter, namely the divergent practices among experimental economists about what unit of data is called "an experiment." While this divergence is sometimes merely a matter of terminology, it sometimes masks differences in reporting practices that can lead to ambiguity about what is being reported.

What is "An Experiment?"

I will focus on two approaches to reporting laboratory experiments that have emerged in the economics literature. They do not exhaust the range of approaches, indeed many reported experiments fall between them. But I think the difference between these two approaches, and their different strengths and limitations, have not been as widely appreciated as they need to be, and that this may contribute to some ongoing controversies in experimental economics.

The first approach, which I will call the method of *planned experimental design*, is the approach that has received the most formal attention in other experimental sciences. In it, investigators fill in the cells of an experimental design. Each *cell* of the experiment consists of *trials* conducted with some fixed set of experimental conditions, and the experimental design specifies which conditions will be varied, and what settings will be observed. The whole set of observations is what is referred to as the "experiment," and these observations are reported and analyzed together. There is a large literature on different kinds of experimental design, i.e. on different ways of identifying the effects of particular variables.

For example, when we speak of an experiment that uses a 3×2 factorial design, we mean one in which there are two experimental variables, one of which is observed at 3 settings and one of which is observed at 2 settings, and in which all 6 combinations of these settings are observed. (It is often impractical to employ factorial designs, which look at all combinations. Many experiments examine only some subset of the possible cells.) Each trial of the experiment consists of an observation at a particular pair of settings (and may be a complicated event involving many transactions by many subjects), and each cell of the experiment consists of independent trials at the same choice of settings. The data of the experiment consist of all the trials in all the cells examined.

Under this approach, once an experiment has been designed and conducted, few if any questions of judgement arise about what data to report. Although the deletion of occasional data points from the analysis may be noted with the explanation that they were outliers, or that some breakdown of the experimental procedures took place in the trial in which they were collected, the presumption is that all the data collected are reported.

This does not mean that there are not ways in which judgement may have played a role that needs to be communicated if the experiment is to be properly understood. While it is obviously a matter of judgement what experiments to conduct, i.e. which conditions to vary and what parameters to set, what is less obvious because it is often unreported is how these decisions might have been influenced by preliminary "pilot" experiments that may have been run. This is where the question of unreported search may arise. I will return to this subject, and why I think there is room for improvement in the way we report these matters, after introducing the second approach to reporting experiments that has become common in the literature.

In what I will call the method of *independent trials*, each trial is itself regarded as an experiment. The inclination to do this in economics experiments arises from the fact that each trial may be a complex event consisting of multiple decisions and observations[2]. But when each trial is regarded as a separate experiment, the potential for problems associated with unreported matters of judgement is magnified, because even the question of what trials to report, or to report together in the same paper, may be taken to be a matter of judgement[3]. This kind of problem is further magnified in an active laboratory which may

[2] For example, allowing subjects to participate in many repetitions of a given market may be desirable, to allow them to gain experience of market parameters and of the behavior of others.

[3] Some additional confusion is caused by the fact that even some experimenters who conduct and report planned experimental designs have started to follow the practice of calling each trial an experiment. But this confusion can be fixed just by a change in terminology, since these experimenters are simply reporting all the data in their design.

have related investigations proceeding simultaneously, since then the problem of sorting which trials to present as evidence bearing on a particular question may be decided only when the time comes to write a formal report. And the distinction between which trials are pilot experiments and which trials are "actual" experiments may become entirely arbitrary.

The potential for trouble in treating each trial as an independent experiment depends on the kind of conclusions the experimenter seeks to draw from the data. One relatively *un*troublesome use of the method of independent trials in experimental economics is in investigations intended to show that some theory is not a good predictor for every situation to which it might be thought to apply, i.e. investigations intended to find counterexamples.

A good example is the famous "paradox" of Allais (1953). To establish that there are some risky choices for which expected utility theory is not a good predictor, Allais reported two pairs of lotteries for which a substantial percentage of subjects, when faced with the task of choosing one lottery from each pair, made choices inconsistent with expected utility theory. This is a reliable result: you can present a pair of lotteries like Allais' to your class in the confident expectation that many of your students will make the choices that Allais observed. Subsequent experimenters have considerably expanded the kinds of lotteries about which this can be said, and they customarily report these as independent trials. That is, it is customary to report tasks for which subjects consistently violate expected utility theory without reporting the entire set of tasks that the experimenter may have examined.

In this case it is not clear that much information is lost by this practice. Suppose the task reported by some investigator, which shows subjects violating expected utility theory, were the result of a search in which he presented ten different tasks to subjects, and that the responses to the other nine tasks were largely consistent with utility theory. We cannot conclude from this anything about the percentage of cases in which expected utility theory will be unreliable: another experimenter, with less insight, might have had to search through a hundred choice tasks before finding a good counterexample, and yet another investigator might have found the same example on his first try.

A more problematic use of the method of independent trials involves the search for examples that illustrate a theory. Such examples are sometimes thought of as constructive proofs that the theory is not behaviorally vacuous, i.e. as demonstrations that the theory applies at least in some observable situations. Suppose an investigator is interested in finding a game in which a certain kind of equilibrium outcome can be observed, and that, using the method of independent trials he examines ten games, identifies one in which the equilibrium is regularly observed, and reports only that one. (Since he regards each trial as an independent experiment, he regards those trials involving the other nine games as unrelated, failed experiments[4].) Even if the investigator has no

[4] But note that there are circumstances in which even an investigator intending to report a planned experimental design might come to regard the other games as pilot experiments: suppose

intention of implying that this kind of equilibrium will be reached in all games, some information is lost when the nine games in which non-equilibrium outcomes were observed go unreported. In particular, there might be some common process that accounts for the outcomes of all ten games, and which coincides with the equilibrium outcome of the one reported game merely by accident. Including a brief account of the other nine games could give clues to other investigators, while a failure to report them could easily lead astray even investigators seeking to follow up on the reported experiment with new experiments, if they stick too closely to games with the structure of the single reported game. My point is that, while there can be very good reasons to carefully select experimental tasks and conditions through search or other means, the manner in which this selection is carried out is a reportable part of the experiment.

The most troublesome use of the method of independent trials is when the investigator interprets his data as supporting the general predictions of some theory, such as a theory which says that all games will result in a certain kind of equilibrium outcome. If trials in which the theory fails are not reported together with those in which it succeeds, an entirely erroneous impression about the success of the theory can be given[5].

What can we Learn from the Experimental Traditions in Other Sciences?

The first thing that becomes apparent from the experimental traditions of other sciences is that there seems to be no foolproof way to set guidelines for what constitutes "all the relevant data" from an experimental investigation. When the National Academy of Science's Committee on the Conduct of Science at-

---

each game is initially examined with just a few subjects, and only in five of the games are some equilibrium outcomes observed. These five games are then examined with a few more subjects, and only in one of them does the equilibrium outcome occur with really high frequency. Finally that one game is examined with more subjects and reported, with some parametric variations, as part of a small experimental design focused on the one game. The investigator regards the other games as failed pilot experiments, and doesn't report them.

[5] In this connection I once had the opportunity to hear one experimental economist chide another for having reported that a certain kind of market did not always yield equilibrium behavior. He felt that perhaps a premature negative result had been reported. He went on to say that, in his own research, when he found in an experiment that some economic institution "didn't work," he first tried rewriting the instructions to make sure that they hadn't contributed to the negative result, and if that didn't fix the problem he would try changing the mechanics of the experiment. Often, he said, that fixed the problem. Left unstated was that this search for conditions that would yield the desired result was not reported in the papers that resulted from this activity, which simply presented, as if they were independent experiments, trials that had "worked."

tempted to describe how data should be treated, they noted this difficulty with the following cautiously worded story (1989, pp2–3):

"One well-known example of this difficulty involves the physicist Robert Millikan, who won the Nobel Prize in 1923 for his work on the charge of the electron. In the 1910s, just as most physicists were coming to accept the existence of the electron, Millikan carried on a protracted and sometimes heated dispute with the Viennese physicist Felix Ehrenhaft over the magnitude of the smallest electrical charge found in nature ... Ehrenhaft used all the observations he made, without much discrimination and eventually concluded that there was no lower limit to the size of an electrical charge that could exist in nature. Millikan used only what he regarded as his 'best' data sets to establish the magnitude of the charge and argue against the existence of Ehrenhaft's 'subelectrons.' In other words, Millikan applied methods of data selection to his observations that enabled him to demonstrate the unitary charge of the electron.

"Millikan has been criticized for not disclosing which data he omitted or why he omitted those data. But an examination of his notebooks reveals that Millikan felt he knew just how far he could trust his raw data. He often jotted down in his notebooks what he thought were good reasons for excluding data. However, he glossed over these exclusions in some of his published papers, and by present standards this is not acceptable."

It is of course difficult to judge particular cases, especially in hindsight once the phenomena in question seem well understood. Elsewhere in the same document (p14) the Committee on the Conduct of Science characterize as fraud the deliberate practice of "selecting only those data that support a hypothesis and concealing the rest ('cooking' data)."[6] What is clear is that the larger the role that unreported "methods of data selection" play in determining what data are presented, the harder it is for readers to reliably interpret the data.

Another theme that stands out in the experimental literature is that experimenters must constantly guard against self deception: particularly when an investigator has clear intuitions about what should happen, it is easy to read these into the data[7]. Many of the specialized experimental methods commonly employed in some sciences (e.g. double blind trials) are addressed directly at such problems. And much of the general aim of experimental methodology is to reduce the scope for the subjective expectations of the investigators to play a critical role.

In summary, one method of data selection that is clearly beyond the pale is to select only data that conform to the predictions of the hypothesis being (nominally) tested. But this is not a simple thing to guard against when procedures are used in which experimenters' subjective expectations may play a large role. Many experimental methods, including the use of planned experimental designs, are intended to guard against inadvertently selecting data in this way.

---

[6] In medical research, where each trial may involve a separate laboratory animal, for example, I have heard the practice of treating each trial as an independent experiment and reporting only those that support the hypothesis referred to as "forgetting about the mouse that died."

[7] There have even been experiments aimed at elucidating this effect. For example, Rosenthal and Fode [1963] show in a controlled experiment that experimenters who were told that a given rat was experienced or inexperienced at running a maze reported results that reflected their expectations.

The Potential for Mis-Communication due to Different Theoretical Predispositions

A subsequent committee of the National Academy of Sciences, the Panel on Scientific Responsibility and the Conduct of Research, quotes the historian Jan Sapp as follows

> "What 'liberties' scientists are allowed in selecting positive data and omitting conflicting or 'messy' data from their reports is not defined by any timeless method. It is a matter of negotiation. It is learned, acquired socially; scientists make judgments about what fellow scientists might expect in order to be convincing. What counts as good evidence may be more or less well-defined after a new discipline or specialty is formed; however, at revolutionary stages in science, when new theories and techniques are being put forward, when standards have yet to be negotiated, scientists are less certain as to what others may require of them to be deemed competent and convincing." (Sapp, 1990, p113 as quoted in NAS, 1992, p39.)

Experimental economics is certainly a relatively new technique in economic research (despite tracing its origins back over sixty years, see Roth, 1993 or Roth, forthcoming), and the rapidly growing acceptance of experimental evidence undoubtedly constitutes something of a revolution, so in light of the above quotation it should not surprise us to find that the views I have outlined here do not meet with complete agreement (recall footnote 5).

The essence of the position I have taken is that negative results, i.e. results contrary to the experimenter's expectations or to received theory, are potentially very informative, and ought to be reported even if the experimenter decides to pursue results more in accord with his expectations or with standard theory. But what one investigator may view as informative results contrary to the predictions of received theory may be seen by another investigator as a failed experiment. For example, I have seen it argued that an experiment to detect a Nash equilibrium is like an experiment to detect a subatomic particle, and that once it has been reliably detected in one experiment, experiments which fail to detect it can be regarded as failures[8].

Now I certainly don't want to discourage scientists who believe that their experimental apparatus is defective from tinkering with it until it works better. (In an economic experiment, this might involve changing the instructions to the subjects, the mechanics of the experiment, some parameters, or even the game or market being investigated.) My point is that there is room for substantial

---

[8] For the record, I do not agree with the hypothesis that if one game is observed to reach equilibrium it must therefore follow that other games, even similar games, do also, nor do I agree that disequilibrium observations imply an error in the experiment or the analysis. In fact I have reported experiments designed to explore why some games move quickly to their subgame perfect equilibrium while others do not (see Prasnikar and Roth, 1992, Roth, Prasnikar, Okuno-Fujiwara, and Zamir, 1991, and see Roth and Erev, 1993 for a theoretical treatment.) However it is not my intention to discuss the merits of these hypotheses here.

miscommunication if the search for conditions that yield the desired result is not reported in the resulting papers, which instead present as evidence only those trials that "succeeded," and do not mention the nature of the "failures" and the search for conditions which avoided them.

Concluding Remarks

For a variety of reasons, experimental economists have often found that the phenomena they wish to explore, and the hypotheses they wish to test, require experiments in which each trial is a complex event, which may involve many separate transactions. And because of the technology of economics experiments, trials tend to be conducted sequentially rather than (as in agriculture experiments) simultaneously. Perhaps for these reasons, there has been a tendency among some experimental economists to regard each trial as a separate experiment. This practice greatly increases the potential for data selection to play a primary role in the analysis and interpretation of experimental results, and consequently for investigators' subjective expectations to influence the data they report. And when the procedures and parameters for the experimental trials ultimately selected for reporting are influenced by unreported pilot experiments, the process may come to bear more than a passing resemblance to the kind of search about which Leamer (1983) alerted econometricians.

This latter comment can also apply to experiments reported according to a planned experimental design. And under either method, the questions of what experiments to conduct, and which experiments to report together and which separately (and which not at all) are questions of art, as opposed to matters of clearly defined practice. The difference between the two methods, then, has to do with the fact that the method of independent trials, by considering each trial to be an experiment, makes *all* the decisions about data presentation questions of art, while the method of planned design restricts this artistic freedom by requiring the experimenter to first report the design (i.e. all the observations to be made in the experiment), and then to report all of these observations, and to report them together. Insofar as all experimenters need to take care not to let their prior expectations play too great a role in determining which parts of the data they take seriously, experimenters who regard each trial as a separate experiment may want to reconsider whether this is the best approach for the questions they wish to address. And to avoid unnecessary confusion, experimenters who are reporting all the data in their design should probably avoid calling each trial an experiment[9].

[9] It is a simple matter to speak of trials, or experimental "sessions", rather than "experiments" in such a case.

There is room for us all to do a better job reporting what kind of pilot experiments we have conducted, and how they may have influenced the design choices made in the experiments from which the reported data were gathered. It may not always be possible or desirable to conduct pre-planned experimental designs, as the results in an early cell of an experiment may call for a change in plans. But if the process by which the data are collected is reported, the potential for miscommunication can be reduced.

As in econometric research, we may draw different inferences about the robustness of results that result from a search[10]. In this connection, we should also, as editors and referees, give some thought to making sure that we do not create incentives that encourage poor reporting practices. This is not a simple thing, for it means both showing a tolerance for ambiguity of results in well designed experiments, and being prepared to publish replications of various sorts, particularly those aimed at investigating the robustness of conclusions[11].[12] But the experience of other fields suggests that there is a limit to what can be accomplished by exhortation of authors or editors. As a profession, our best defense

---

[10] To further the analogy with econometrics, the standard error of a (single) regression which is selected from a search understates the ambiguity of the data, and may be a biased estimator. In just such a way, experimental evidence that results from a search through conditions understates the ambiguity of the evidence, and may misrepresent the data, if it omits mention of the search. A related matter is that, because trials are often costly, and because they may involve multiple decisions by subjects who interact with one another in complicated ways, even planned experimental designs for economic experiments often have relatively few cells, few trials per cell, and few truly independent observations per trial. There is room for improved econometric techniques for the analysis of such data. And, here too, replication of results plays a vital role. (Replication in experimental economics means a very different thing than it does in econometrics, where it sometimes refers to the ability of other investigators simply to reproduce the same analyses from the same data – see Dewald, Thursby, and Anderson, 1986. Experimenters seek to replicate a result by generating new data under the same or comparable conditions.)

[11] Writing about the applied econometrics literature, Feige (1975), in the paper which caused the *Journal of Political Economy* to start accepting papers in the category "Confirmations and Contradictions," wrote:

"... current journal editorial policies have undoubtedly contributed to (1) an incentive to pursue search procedures for statistically significant results which are spurious as often reported, insofar as they take no account of pretest bias; (2) an incentive for less than candid reporting of intermediate results which could highlight the lack of robustness of statistical tests to alternative model specifications and applications of alternative econometric techniques; (3) an underrepresentation of "negative" results which could otherwise signal empirically anomalous results leading to the rejection of currently maintained hypotheses; and (4) an unnoticed proliferation of published Type 1 errors." (pp1292–93).

[12] Counterproductive incentives about what to report may also exist in areas of economics involving other than econometric or experimental data. I have only an anecdote to offer about economic history, having to do with a forthcoming paper of mine (Roth and Xing, 1994) which contains historical descriptions of the evolution of the timing of transactions in several dozen markets, along with some theoretical models of the observed phenomena. One reviewer suggested that the historical data exhibited an excess variety of behavior compared to that which could be accounted for by the formal theoretical models. Obviously one way to avoid such a criticism would be to report only those historical observations that can be explained by the available theory.

against erroneous conclusions resulting from unreported or incompletely reported search is to encourage experimenters to follow up on one another's work, with experiments which change elements of the design that might influence the outcome in ways not accounted for by the theory or theories proposed to account for the results.

Indeed, one of the reasons that experimental economics has been as productive as it has is that reported results have by and large been straightforwardly replicable: when a carefully conducted experiment is repeated, the likelihood that the data will be similar seems to be high. But precise replication gives little information about robustness. What ultimately gives us our best indication of the robustness of experimental results is replication with some variation of experimental parameters and conditions. And, particularly in the last ten years as experimental economists have become numerous enough so that investigators with different theoretical predispositions have started to examine the same questions, we have seen that investigators with different intuitions about a question can sometimes design experiments that lead them to different conclusions. In this respect, some of the controversies in the experimental literature focus on questions of robustness, and will be more productively carried out when methodological issues concerning how much search has been conducted and how much data selection has been employed are clearly reported.

In conclusion, one of the principal roles of experimental methodology is to help investigators avoid the danger of too easily accepting their prior hypotheses. The experience of other sciences suggests that this is a problem that will be always with us: evidence counter to the preferred hypothesis may look like experimental error ("the subjects didn't understand"), there is a natural tendency to keep trying different parameters when things aren't working out, but to stick with parameters which do work out, etc. As in econometric research, experimental results which are the end product of a search for conditions and parameters that will yield certain kinds of results are difficult to interpret without some understanding of the search process. And all of these problems are exacerbated when investigators regard each trial as an independent experiment.

But overall, the experimental enterprise contains many elements that promote the identification of robust results. Chief among these is that experimenters don't have to rely on one anothers' data, or even their choices of parameters and procedures, but can generate their own data from experimental environments well suited to testing their hypotheses precisely. And so *series* of experiments allow the experimental community to build upon and critique one anothers' work in ways that are not as readily available to economists using non-experimental methods. There is every reason for optimism about the contribution that series of experiments, particularly when conducted by experimenters with different points of view who take care to address each others' positions, can make to identifying robust empirical regularities in economics[13].

---

[13] For many fine examples of the success of this approach, see the forthcoming *Handbook of Experimental Economics* (Kagel and Roth, forthcoming).

The purpose of this note is to help to enhance the efficiency of this kind of dialogue, by raising some of the methodological issues that both producers and consumers of experimental research must consider in interpreting experimental results.

References

Allais M (1953) Le comportement de l'homme rationnel devant le risque: Critique des postulats et axiomes de l'ecole Americane. Econometrica 21:503–546

Dewald WG, Thursby JG, Anderson RG (1986) Replication in empirical economics: The journal of money, credit and banking project. American Economic Review 76:587–603

Feige EL (1975) The consequences of journal editorial policies and a suggestion for revision. Journal of Political Economy 83:1291–1295

Kagel JH, Roth AE (Eds) Handbook of experimental economics. Princeton University Press, forthcoming

Leamer EE (1983) Let's take the con out of econometrics. American Economic Review 73:31–43

National Academy of Sciences (1989) On being a scientist. Committee on the Conduct of Science, Washington, National Academy Press

National Academy of Sciences (1992) Responsible science: Ensuring the integrity of the research process, Volume I. Panel on scientific responsibility and the conduct of research. Washington, National Academy Press.

Prasnikar V, Roth AE (1992) Considerations of fairness and strategy: Experimental data from sequential games. Quarterly Journal of Economics 865–888

Rosenthal R, Fode KL (1963) The effect of experimenter bias on the performance of the albino rat. Behavioral Science 8:183–189

Roth AE (1993) On the early history of experimental economics. Journal of the History of Economic Thought 15:184–209.

Roth AE (1994) Introduction to experimental economics. Chapter 1 of Handbook of experimental economics, Kagel J, Roth AE (Eds) Princeton University Press, forthcoming

Roth AE, Erev I (1993) Learning in extensive-form games: Experimental data and simple dynamic models in the intermediate term. Mimeo, presented at the Nobel Symposium on Game Theory, June 18–20, Bjorkborn, Sweden

Roth AE, Prasnikar V, Okuno-Fujiwara M, Zamir S (1991) Bargaining and market behavior in Jerusalem, Ljubljana, Pittsburgh, and Tokyo: An experimental study. American Economic Review 81:1068–1095

Roth AE, Xing X. Jumping the gun: Imperfections and institutions related to the timing of market transactions. American Economic Review, forthcoming

Sapp J (1990) Where the truth lies: Franz Moewus and the origins of molecular biology. Cambridge, Cambridge University Press

Experiments in Multi-Stage R&D Competition

PATRIZIA SBRIGLIA AND JOHN D. HEY[1]

Department of Economics, University of York, Heslington, York YO1 5DD, United Kingdom

JEL-Classification System-Numbers: C92, D21

Introduction

In this paper we present the results from a series of experiments dealing with R&D competition. The aim of the experiments was to provide some insights into how firms search for innovations that will allow them to gain significant profits, as in the case of patentable innovations, and how they adjust their search strategies in order to take account of the competition from other potential innovators. Other aspects examined by our experiments were how firms (subjects) distributed their spending over the periods their search lasted, what use they made of information on their own performance and on that of their competitors, and what elements were likely to influence their decision to enter the competition or to drop out.

There exist a considerable number of contributions to the theory of patent races. Particular interest has been devoted to understanding how the experience accumulated by firms during the race affects the pace of their innovative activity, that is to say, how firms vary the speed of their investment, as they progress in the development of the patentable innovation, and how the research investment rate is affected by competition. These models, although revealing important aspects of the problem, do not provide a satisfactory framework in which real world R&D races can be studied.

R&D activity is a very complex phenomenon. When competing for a patent, innovative firms face a multi-dimensional problem. The first aspect concerns the search activity of the innovative firms. If an innovation can be developed by pursuing different research patterns, firms have to choose from among the possible alternatives the one that gives the highest probability of success, with a minimum cost and development time. The second aspect regards the firms' ability and skill in implementing the chosen search procedures. Research abilities differ in the real world, some firms being more efficient – or better innovators – than others. Such characteristics influence the research outcomes and the

[1] Patrizia Sbriglia thanks the Fondazione Ivo Vanzi (Napoli) for financing a substantial part of the experiments, and the CNR for financial support during her visit to the University of York. We thank Norman Spivey of EXEC for providing the networked software for the experiments, and the EXEC staff – Cristina Pitassi and Gianna Lotito – for assistance during the experiments.

investment rate, as well as the willingness to participate in the R&D competition in the first place. The third aspect regards the investment decision: firms have to decide whether to start the R&D activity, when and whether to drop out of the race, and the speed of investment over time.

Presumably, one would wish to model the R&D activity of innovative firms as a decision problem in which more agents are involved, or more departments within the same firms' structure. The way however such decisions are formed and affected by market competitors is still to be studied and many insights may be gained by using experimental methods. We constructed an experiment in which subjects had to deal with a particular search problem (the discovery of an unknown combination of elements), whose solution might guarantee a significant profit, while competing with other players. The experiments produced a rich data set, regarding the search procedures chosen by the players, the economic decisions related to each particular search procedure, and the role played by the information structure.

The main results concern the patterns of behaviour of different players (winners and losers). In all experiments, the winners applied a successful search procedure and did not play randomly (although in one set of experiments luck played an important role). Generally, they invested more than their participation fee and more than the other participants (two cases excluded). In the presence of a low search cost, uncertain information on performance and small number of competitors, the winners invested at a lower speed, the number of rounds which the game lasted increased and successful players were willing to change search procedures as their experience improved. Competition speeded up investment in research and in the monopoly case (one subject left to play) the research spending proceeded at the lowest speed. Competition and negative expected profit from joint discovery increased the rate of investment in the first round and decreased the number of rounds the game lasted. The spending rate of the winner in this case closely resembles the pre-emptive behaviour of the dominant firm, as analysed by Gilbert and Newbery (1982). The pattern of behaviour of losers was more difficult to classify. Unskilled players who did not have any search strategy or did not succeed in implementing one, invested at a low rate per round, while losers who had a successful search procedure but invested at a lower rate than the winner (or were less lucky) had a similar behaviour to the latter. Finally, the information structure played a crucial role for the decision as to whether to quit the race. On the effects of competition on R&D investment, our experiments confirm some of the relevant results already existing in the literature; to these, the experimental design allows us to add the examination of how different innovative skills and ability influence the outcome of the race.

Because of the many aspects considered in our experiments, this is mainly an exploratory study in the area of R&D competition, where we believe there is still a significant gap between theory, empirical analysis and real world phenomena. We tried to reduce this gap by providing a simple but realistic experimental setup in which technological R&D competition can be studied.

The paper is organized as follows. Section 1 reviews some of the literature on patent races. Section 2 presents the experimental evidence on R&D competition and describes the aims of our experiments. In Section 3, the experimental design of the Combination Race is presented, while in Section 4 the methods applied by successful players, or "innovators", in order to find the unknown (winning) combination are presented. Search procedures of unsuccessful players are also compared and classified. Section 5 describes the results of the experiments, as far as entry/exit decisions and spending patterns. In Section 6 we carry out a simulation study to examine whether Nash equilibrium behaviour in this game would be compatible with the actual behaviours followed by the subjects during the experiments. For a sub-set of experiments a Nash equilibrium in pure strategy can be characterised, and the actual behaviour of our player corresponded to the equilibrium strategy only for 5 players out of 20. Finally, in the conclusion we discuss possible extensions to our study.

1 Patent Races

A patent race is a particular form of competition in which potential innovators compete for the introduction of a new technology, but. only the firm which produces the innovation first is awarded a patent, which protects it from imitation or duplication for a period of time. If the patent protection is perfect, and the innovative know-how is non-transferable, competition among potential innovators takes the form of a race, in which "the winner takes all".

The importance of patenting as a way of protecting the returns from R&D investment varies among industries, and only in some cases is patenting regarded as the best way to appropriate the returns from the new technology[2]. However, competition among potential innovators takes the form of a race also when lead time in marketing the innovation is important and in all other cases in which the innovator can prevent other firms from reaping the profits from the innovation, bearing a lower cost of production. In every R&D investment decision of potential innovators, uncertainty plays a major role. The innovative and inventive activity has of necessity an uncertain outcome, in as much as the firm cannot predict the final date of discovery and therefore its ability to gain the patent. For these reasons, most models on patent races concentrate on the technical and market uncertainty related to the R&D process.

[2] For empirical evidence on this point, see Mansfield et al. (1981) and Levin et al. (1984). Scherer (1980) contains a wide discussion and analysis of the costs and benefits of the patent system.

A well known context in which patent races have been studied is the stochastic racing model[3], analysed in the works of Loury (1979), Lee and Wilde (1980), Dasgupta and Stiglitz (1980b) and Grossman and Shapiro (1987). In the single period stochastic racing model, by investing in R&D an amount of resources x_i, firms select a random variable, $\tau(x_i)$, representing the date of completion, which is distributed exponentially[4]. Firms maximize the expected discounted profits from R&D investment, for values of the revenue flow, V, in the case of winning, the discount rate, r, and the aggregate rival hazard rate, $a = \sum_{j \neq i} h(x_j)$.[5] The analysis of the noncooperative equilibrium of this game gives relevant results. First, the research intensity of the individual firm (and of the overall industry) increases with the number of firms participating in the race. With increased R&D investment, both the firm $((1/h(x^*))$ and the industry $((1/nh(x^*))$ expected dates of completion are reduced.[6]. Second, for a given n, in equilibrium each firm invests at a higher rate than is jointly optimal. Overinvestment in the noncooperative equilibrium is also proved for an industry with unrestricted entry.

The stochastic racing model leaves many questions unanswered. The first question is related to the strategic advantage that the leader in the race has on the firms which are lagging behind and how this particular advantage can affect the amount of resources that leaders and followers are prepared to commit in order to win the prize. The point can be explained as follows. In the single period patent race firms choose a research intensity (or an investment level) at the outset, and this cannot be varied during the race. In real world R&D competition, we can observe that being the leader or the follower may imply completely different speeds of investment. The follower, for instance, may speed up with the intention of catching up or of leapfrogging the leader, or may decide to drop out if he reckons he has little chance of catching up the leader and winning. The different research efforts of asymmetrically placed firms reflect the role that

---

[3] See Reinganum, 1989, for an extensive survey on the literature on patent races.

[4] The probability that firm i completes the innovation by t_i is: $Pr(\tau(x_i) \leq t) = 1 - \exp\{-h(x_i)\}$, where $h(x_i)$ is the (conditional) instantaneous probability of success or *hazard rate*. $h(x_i)$ represents the R&D technology and is assumed to be twice differentiable and strictly increasing. The assumption used in the models of patent races is that there are diminishing returns to scale in the innovation technology. Notice also that the expected date of completion is given by $E\,\tau(x_i) = 1/h(x_i)$.

[5] We consider the hypothesis of non-contractual costs introduced by Lee and Wilde and widely adopted in subsequent studies on patent races. According to this version, firms choose a R&D investment rate (or intensity) until one of the firms participating in the race succeeds. The alternative hypothesis (Loury, Dasgupta and Stiglitz) considered contractual costs: R&D is viewed as a lump sum expenditure to which firms are committed regardless of whether the innovation is introduced by any of the rivals (say, R&D regards the choice of the number of the research labs). The two versions yield in some cases conflicting results.

[6] This result is partly reversed in Loury's model, since an increase in the number of firms decreases in equilibrium the individual level of investment and decreases the individual expected date of completion. This is an important point of conflict, because it implies a completely different story about the effect of industrial concentration on R&D investment.

learning (as accumulation of experience), in terms of information on performance, has in deciding who wins the race. This issue has been examined by models of multi-stage races, in which firms compete over a number of stages to discover a single innovation. The simplest way to analyse the strategic advantage of the leading firm is to consider a straightforward extension of the Lee and Wilde model to a two stage competition, as in Grossman and Shapiro (1987). Consider an innovation that needs two different production phases: basic research and development. Completing the first stage does not yield any intrinsic payoff except the opportunity to get closer to the final line[7]. There are two firms competing for the patent that is awarded to the winner that completes the two stages first, and each firm, by investing in R&D, achieves a flow probability, p, of being successful. There are two possible scenarios: (i) both firms are in the first or in the second stage; (ii) one firm (the follower) is in the first stage and the other (the leader) is in the second stage. Notice that if (i) is the case, the game is symmetric and it is simply the Lee and Wilde model for a duopoly. At each point in time, firms maximize the expected value of the investment, which can be defined in each scenario for the leader and the follower in the race, and it is possible to characterize the equilibrium speeds[8] p_{ij} by using backward induction. The main result is that the leading firm invests more than the follower and the highest speed is achieved when both firms are in the second stage. Secondly, firms increase R&D spending when they are close to discovery, and, although the comparison of the speed of leader and follower and the initial speed (p_{00}) gives ambiguous results, simulations suggest that the response to success by one firm in the first stage is for the leader to increase its speed and for the follower to decrease its investment in R&D.

In an alternative framework, Fudenberg et al (1983) and Harris and Vickers (1985) found that competition is fiercer when firms are neck and neck. If one firm lags behind, it drops out as the distance from the leading firm increases[9], if the information lag decreases, a small head start induces the follower to drop out immediately. If the information lag is very short, therefore, a small difference in the initial experience prevents the disadvantaged firm from entering the race at all. Here, distance (or experience) is described as a number of steps which are still to be covered to win the patent. Cost are convex, so that it is optimal to proceed at the lowest speed and firms do so only if the follower drops out and the industry become a monopoly. In Harris and Vickers (1985) the distance is measured not in number of steps but in terms of different evaluations of the patent by firms facing different cost conditions. Although the model provides a

[7] This is a game of perfect information and the concept of equilibrium used is subgame perfect Nash equilibrium.

[8] p_{ij} is the probability of success of a firm which has concluded i stages when its rival has concluded j stages.

[9] In Fudenberg et al. firms observe their opponents performance (distance) with a lag: at time t, firm i is able to observe firm j research efforts at time $t - 1$.

more general setup, the results of Harris and Vickers (1985) closely resemble those obtained by Fudenberg et al.

Finally, one important aspect that has been considered in models of patent races is how *ex ante* monopoly power affects the firms' incentive to invest in R&D and thus in securing the patent. There is no strategic advantage, but the issue here is related to the incentive to undertake innovative activity in oligopolistic and monopolistic industries. This argument dates back to Schumpeter's analysis of innovation and technical change, and in Schumpeter's view oligopolistic industries induce more technical change than competitive ones. Along these lines, auction models like Gilbert and Newbery (1982) have proved that a monopolist will always pre-empt the race, preventing a challenger from entering the market, if the *ex-post* duopoly profits, due to the challenger's entry, are lower than the monopoly profits the firm earns in the pre-innovation market.

Nelson and Winter (1982) and Nelson (1987) examined the relationship between competition and technical change in models in which agents do not follow the optimising paradigm. The main results are that innovation tends to generate aggressive investment behaviour and, in the case of successful R&D strategies, the emergence of dominant firms (with higher concentration in post-innovation market structures) when imitation is impeded and the competitive advantage conferred by the new technology is large. But R&D competition may determine interesting results also when imitation is possible and firms can choose to invest in imitative and/or innovative research activity. When innovation costs are high relative to the prize, aggressive imitators, who face lower costs and reap some of the profits, may lag behind in the innovative activity but force the innovators out of the product market.

2 Experimental Evidence on Patent Races and Aim of the Experiments

There are only a few laboratory experiments conducted on R&D competition. With one exception, most of these experiments have been used to test some of the predictions of existing models of patent races. Isaac and Reynolds (1988) and Hey and Reynolds (1991) are, respectively, experimental tests of the single period stochastic invention model (as in Lee and Wilde (1980)) and the multi-stage model of Fudenberg et al. (1983). Since both papers aim to test whether the Nash equilibrium predictions are confirmed in the laboratory setting, the experimental design is a close reproduction of the theory.

More recently, Isaac and Reynolds (1992) have extended the previous analysis of the stochastic invention model to a more general framework of a two-stage game, in which firms invest in a cost reducing innovation in the first stage, and compete in an oligopolistic product market in the second stage. The experiments confirm the existence of Schumpeterian competition, that is, successful R&D investment in the first stage induces price competition in the second stage, with part of the profits generated by the cost reducing innovation transferred onto consumers.

The application of experimental economics in this area is filling an existing gap between theory and empirical analyses. First, by using laboratory experiments it is possible to verify some of the predictions of the theory, as well as the realism of the assumptions on which the theory is based, in a way that conventional econometric empirical tests cannot be used. Second, and more importantly, experimental economics can help in understanding the effect of variables whose importance needs still to be fully investigated theoretically. We are thinking primarily of the effect of the learning process that takes place during the race. When firms invest in R&D they increase their stock of knowledge at a speed that partly depends on the amount of R&D investment, partly on their own ability and partly on the nature of the problem they are trying to solve. These components of the learning process (R&D spending, ability, nature of the innovation), are essential to every research project and determine also the speed at which innovations are produced and patented. In the theory of multi-stage patent races, however, the complex links between R&D spending, learning and production of innovations are oversimplified. The nature of the innovation itself influences the speed of learning. Innovations can be classified according to the degree of novelty they contain: some of them can be considered "breakthroughs" while some others are much less important. According to which innovative process the firm is facing, the speed of learning varies, as well as the kind of information firms receive on their own performance and on that of their opponents. To the understanding of the determinants of the technological learning, much empirical work has been devoted in recent years, and the aim of the experiments we present in the following sections is to examine how the learning process generated by a particular search activity (discovering an unknown combination of elements) is affected by the subjects' ability in solving the specific problem, by the nature of the innovation and by the competition with other potential innovators.

Specifically, three aspects of the problem have been examined with our laboratory investigations:

– *Selection of Search Procedures:* we were interested in observing what search procedures the players selected in order to solve the problem, and whether they changed them as a response to changes in the characteristics of the environment in which they are competing.

– *Investment Strategies:* in a race there are winner(s) and losers: we wanted to observe what kind of investment strategies corresponded to each search procedures selected. In other words, do skilled players invest at a higher speed than unskilled ones?

– *Use of Information:* finally, we were interested in observing what use the players made of the information given during the race and whether different structures of information affected the selection of procedures and the investment strategies the players chose.

3 The Experimental Design: The Combination Race

In general terms, the experiments were designed as "innovation races", that is, they described a market situation in which N subjects were competing to discover an unknown combination of elements, which represented the "patentable innovation". The value of the discovery was the prize, V, awarded to the winner of the competition; if more than one subject discovered the unknown combination at the same time, the prize would be shared equally among the "innovators". The remaining participants to the race would bear the costs of their search and gain only what remained from the participation fee allocated to them at the beginning of the experiment (the participants were allowed to continue the search with their own money when the fee was spent).

More specifically, the unknown combination was represented by n letters of the alphabet selected at random without replacement from a set of m.[10] The position of the letters in the winning combination was unimportant. In order to find the combination, subjects were allowed to buy trial combinations of n letters from the organizers and to check with them, at the end of each round, how many correct elements they had guessed in each of their trials[11]. Subjects were also informed, during the race, about the performance of the other participants: on request, they could look at a table that indicated the number of correct elements guessed by each player during the previous rounds. By "rounds" was meant a fixed period of time during which the subject chose the trial combinations, typed them into a computer, received for each trial combination the relevant information and considered the course of action to take in the following round.

Obviously, the information structure played a crucial role. In an innovation race, there are two types of relevant information for the players: the first one is relative to his or her own performance and the second one is relative to his or her opponents' performance. Both kinds of information are likely to influence the spending and the exit decisions.

[10] The experimental design aimed to reproduce, in a very simple fashion, a research process of the kind biochemists might follow. The industry that could be considered closest to this particular type of R&D programmes is the pharmaceutical sector.

[11] Examples of trial combinations participants could buy are: ABCDEFG, HJILMNB, QWERTYU, etc. Subjects were not allowed to buy combination were letters were repeated (e.g., AASSEER).

According to what players were told about their own performance, we designed two basic versions of the Combination Race: deterministic information and noisy information.

In the deterministic information version, each subject could buy trial combinations at a constant and known cost per combination c_1. At the end of the round, the subject received correct information on how many letters were correct in each trial (for example, the message displayed was ABCDEFG 3). In the second version, however, the information was given with noise, the precise implementation being as follows: if the correct number of letters in a trial combination was j then the subject was told that i of them were correct, where the relationship between i and j was[12]:

$$0 < j < n \qquad \begin{cases} & j-1 \quad \text{with prob } 0.25 \\ i = j & \qquad \text{with prob } 0.5 \\ & j+1 \quad \text{with prob } 0.25 \end{cases}$$

$$j = 0 \qquad \left\{ i = \begin{matrix} 0 & \text{with prob } 0.75 \\ 1 & \text{with prob } 0.25 \end{matrix} \right.$$

$$j = n \qquad \left\{ i = \begin{matrix} n-1 & \text{with prob } 0.25 \\ n & \text{with prob } 0.75 \end{matrix} \right.$$

Furthermore, in the "noisy" version, a distinction was made between trial combinations and "declarations". The presence of the random component made it impossible for the subject to detect the correct combination at the checking stage. A further and necessary step was to declare it[13], bearing a constant and known cost of c_2 ($c_2 > c_1$). The "noisy information" design aimed to capture possible changes in the spending strategy, as well as in the search procedures, due to the more uncertain environment in which players were competing.

The values of the parameters V, N, n, m, c_1 and c_2 varied according to the particular implementation considered. A complete list of the values of the parameters is given in Table 1.

Table 1. Combination race I, II, III

	V	N	n	m	c_1	c_2
Type I (deter.info.)	25	5	7	26	10p	
Type II (deter.info.)	25	5	7	26	30p	
Type III	35	5	7	26	10p	20p

[12] These relationships were specified in the instructions given to particpants before the experiments took place. A copy of the instructions is reproduced in the Appendix.

[13] The answer to the player's declarations was of the yes/no type. The subject, therefore, was not informed on how many letters were correct in the declared combination, but only whether it was the winning one or not.

4 How to Solve the Combination Race: Procedures Applied by Successful Players

The experimental design of the Combination Race describes a combinatorial problem of a specific form. Subjects were required to find a successful search procedure that solved such a problem, and for each successful procedure, to minimize the number of rounds, r, and the search cost, C_i, in order to take account of competition. The first part of the problem is therefore to detect what successful procedures can be applied (even in the absence of competition), and were actually applied by players during the experiments, and the second part is to examine the economic implication of the interaction between potential innovators[14].

Let us consider the combinatorial problem and its solutions first. In experiments of Type I and II, the methods that were successfully applied during the experiments followed what can be defined as "the overlapping rule", while in some of the tests and Pilot studies also an alternative procedure emerged[15]. The "overlapping rule" consists in constructing strings of seven letters of which a group of variable size (from 1 to 6 letters) is kept constant. The example below shows the six possible ways in which the "overlapping rule" can be implemented.

A	B	C	D	E	F
over-lapping by 6	over-lapping by 5	over-lapping by 4	over-lapping by 3	over-lapping by 2	over-lapping by 1
ABCDEFG	ABCDEFG	ABCDEFG	ABCDEFG	ABCDEFG	ABCDEFG
BCDEFGH	CDEFGHI	DEFGHIJ	EFGHIJK	FGHIJKL	GHIJKLM
CDEFGHI	EFGHIJK	HIJKLMN	IJKLMNO	KLMNOPQ	MNOPQRS

To describe how the rule works, we report below how in race number 9, the winner found the correct combination, applying rule A.

[14] For convenience we keep the two aspects (search procedures and spending decision) separated and describe in this section what rules winners in our experiments applied in order to solve the problem. The analyses of the search procedures would have been irrelevant if all winners had played randomly, but this was never the case: all winners – and some of the losers – "found" a method to solve the combinatorial problem and their spending decision was affected by their ability.

[15] One related issue concerns the existence of an optimal procedure which allows the determindation of the winning combinations in a minimum number of trial combinations, say x^*. By the similarities that this selection problem presents with the working of some well known computer algorithms, it is possible to assume that such procedure could be found and x^* fully specified. This task however is beyond the aims of our work.

1 Unknown Combination: zspudfw

First Round:	abcdefg	2	mnopqrs	2
	bcdefgh	2	nopqrst	2
	cdefghi	2	opqrstu	3
	defghij	2	pqrstuv	3
	efghijk	1	qrstuvw	3
	fghijkl	1	rstuvwx	3
	ghijklm	0	stuvwxy	3
	hijklmn	0	tuvwxya	2
	ijklmno	0	uvwxyab	2
	jklmnop	1	vwxyabc	1
	klmnopq	1	wxyabcd	2
	lmnopqr	1	xyabcde	1
			yabcdef	2
Second Round:	dfpsuwz	7		

By looking at how the information changes across rows, it is possible to assess whether the letters that are progressively excluded and introduced in the string are in the Winning Combination. The different overlapping rules detect (with certainty) the unknown combination with 25 trial combinations. If we define an efficiency criterion on the basis of how the number of failures increases as the number of trial combinations shrinks, we can see from Table 2 that rule A, can be considered as the "best" search procedure among those applied by players. The table reports the results of simulations conducted on the working of the different rules. Rule A was applied in the majority of the experiments (4 out of 7) of Type I and II, and it was actually preferred in the case of high search cost because it allowed the highest probability of success spending a total amount of 20 combinations.

Table 2.

2.1 The Overlapping Rule: 1000 iterations, 25 combinations (15 in the first round, 10 in the second round)

	A	B	C	D	E	F
round 1	141	229	263	235	143	240
round 2	859	771	737	765	857	760

2.2 The Overlapping Rule: 1000 iterations, 25 combinations (10 in the first round, 10 in the second and 5 in the third)

	A	B	C	D	E	F
round 1	2	8	5	5	2	9
round 2	964	791	766	601	843	574
round 3	34	201	229	394	155	417

In some experiments, the winners applied the same rules of solutions but with small differences from that described above. In some cases, players identified strings of letters whose value was zero and used this information in the following rounds.

Alternatively, when the number of unknown letters was less than seven (as in one of the Pilot studies), winners solved the combinatorial problem by constructing strings in which there was no overlapping and comparing the information across different strings. The following examples illustrates how the discovery of a zero changed the procedure chosen by the player and how, when the unknown combination is constituted by a string of three letters, minimising the number of repetition solve the combinatorial problem with just eighteen trial combinations.[16].

2 Unknown Combination: lcfhspa

first round	abcdefg	3	efghijk	2	abchijk	3
second round	klmnopq	2	opqrstu	2	klmrstu	2
	vwxyzdn	0	acegikm	2	oqsuwyz	1
	nprtvxa	2				
third round	vwxyzdo	0	vwxyzdq	0	vwxyzds	1
	vwxyzdi	0	vwxyzdk	0	vwxyzdl	1
	vwxyzde	0	vwxyzdf	1	vwxyzhj	1
	vwxyzdb	0				
fourth round	aflpsch	7	aflpscj	6		

3 Unknown Combination: ezh

first round	abc	0	def	1	ghj	1
	ikl	0	mno	0	pqr	0
	stu	0	vwx	0	yab	0
	adg	0	beh	2	cfj	0
	imp	0	knq	0	lor	0
	svy	0	twa	0	uxb	0
second round	zeh	3				

[16] The first example corresponds to player 4 in Experiment 3, while the second example is derived by one of the tests. Notice that the application of the overlapping rule requires at least 25 trial combinations to detect the right answer with certainty, regardless of the length of the unknown string and the number of letters that are repeated; the method shown in the second example is therefore better in the case of unknown strings of three letters.

The presence of noisy information did not change the procedures chosen by players but influenced their implementation. All players tried to detect a way to overcome the uncertainty of the information signal, and one specific strategy that was most often adopted was to combine more overlapping rules while repeating the same strings several times and concentrating on high and low levels of information. Naturally, not only the winners of the races but also some of the losers adopted the same procedures.

Three different type of losers' behaviour emerged from our experiments. The first type concerned losers who were applying a procedure similar to the ones described above but did not win because some opponent got the answer first. The reasons why these players lost were generally related to wrong spending decisions and/or luck, according to the type of experiment they were playing. The second type of losers concerned players who tried to apply specific search procedures, but did not succeed in implementing them correctly. Finally, a third type of player applied procedures that can be considered as purely random. Some of these players managed to implement a search procedure, while playing, when the race lasted more than two rounds. The information structure had a major role in the selection and in the implementation of the search procedures, since in the experiments with noisy information the number of incompetent and/or unskilled and random players was higher than in the other experiments, and ability was generally mixed with luck[17]. The search cost also affected the selection and the implementation of the procedures, since with low search cost, the race lasted on average a higher number of rounds and more subjects improved their performance while playing. In the following examples, we show the procedures of three losers in experiments with deterministic information: respectively, a random player, an inexperienced player and a loser who was actually applying an overlapping rule but invested less than the winner in that race.

4 Unknown Combination[18]: bskzghd

first round	cejlptv	0	csqmilw	1	aklodfe	2
second round	–					
third round	adxsbhf	4	bynuorh	2		

[17] The experimental data are available on request.
[18] Race 11, subject 3.

5 Unknown Combination[19]*: lcfhspa*

first round	abcdefg	3	bcdefgh	3	cdefghi	3
	defghij	2	efghijk	2	fghijkl	3
	ghijklm	2	hijklmn	2	ijklmno	1
	jklmnop	2	klmnopq	2	rstuvwx	1
	lmnopgr	2				
second round:	hertyab	2	abrtyed	1	rtyhgfe	2
	ertgsqw	2	ityaber	2		
third and fourth round: –						

6 Unknown Combination[20]*: zspudfw*

first round	qwertyu	2	iopasdf	4	ghjklzx	1
	cvbnmqw	1	ertyuio	1	pasdfgh	4
	jklzxcv	1	bnmqwer	1	tyuiopa	2
	sdfghjk	3	lzxcvbn	1	mqwerty	1
	uiopasd	4	fghjklz	2		
second round	sdufqwp	6	sdufqwl	5	sdufpaq	5

In conclusion, the combinatorial problem of the Combination Races was tackled by the subjects during experiments either using procedures like the ones we described above or by proceeding randomly. The first group of subjects is composed of the winner(s) of the competition and by losers who invested less or were less lucky and losers who were unable to implement the procedure they had chosen. Table 3 shows how much each group of players spent in each of the experiments conducted (WP stands for Winning Players, LP for Losing Players, IP for Inexperienced Players and PR for Random Players).

[19] Race 3, subject 2.
[20] Race 9, subject 1.

Table 3. Total number of combinations per strategy

	Combination Race (Type I) WP	LP	IP	PR
race 1	51(*)	0	20	0
race 2	26	0	0	46
race 3	22	23	18	22
race 4	24	17	0	13

(*) data of one player missing because of software failure.

	Combination Race (Type II) WP	LP	IP	PR
race 9	20	17	6	13
race 10	20	0	0	12
race 11	28	0	0	17

	Combination Race (Type III) WP	LP	IP	PR
race 5	0	0	57(3)	65(1)
race 6	74(5)	0	18(1)	28
race 7	23(1)	37(1)	17(1)	29
race 8	63(2)	0	132(3)	0
race 12	30(2)	40	0	41

5 Results

We conducted 15 experiments in total, including 3 pilot studies[21]. Of the 12 experiments, 7 experiments had a deterministic information structure, while 5 experiments had a stochastic information structure.

[21] In addition to the Pilot studies, 6 tests of the software were conducted and in some cases they produced interesting data. The Pilot studies were mainly aimed at testing the calibration of the experiments. In the first Pilot the experiments were calibrated on very simple search procedures, with $n = 3$. Our simulations suggested that the experiments would last 13 rounds, but the Pilot actually lasted 2 rounds and the winners applied a rule that solved the game with just 18 draws. All the Pilot studies and the experiments were computerised and took place at EXEC at the University of York. Furthermore, during the experimental sessions, players were asked to fill in a questionnaire in which they explained in broad terms their search procedures, their spending and entry/exit decisions, and what use they had made of the information relative to the other players' performance. The questionnaire responses are commented on in the following pages.

The 7 experiments of the first kind were divided into 4 of type I (cost of a trial combination of 10p) and 3 of type II (cost of a trial combination of 30p). In experiments of type II, the expected payoff in the case of joint discovery at the beginning of the second round (applying, for instance, an overlapping rule of six) would have been negative (see Section 6).

In all experiments but one, the unknown combination was eventually discovered by one or more players. The length of the game varied between 2 and 24 rounds (the former being the minimum length achieved only with experiments of type I and II, the latter being the maximum length achieved in an experiment of type III).

We observed that the length was affected by the cost, the information structure and the number of competitors. The average length of the experiments of type I was 3 rounds, while the average length of the experiments of type II was 2.3 rounds, with the winner investing more in the first round in order to secure victory directly in the second. Obviously, in the noisy information version, experiments lasted more rounds. In particular, in one case (race 8), when only one subject was left to play, the experiment lasted 24 rounds, with the player buying only a few combinations at each stage. The number of participants varied between 5 and 6 (the latter being the number chosen for the Pilot studies),

Table 4. Total number of combinations (declarations)

	Combination Race (Type I)				
	P1⁺	P2	P3	P4	P5
race 1	(*)	0	25#	26#	20#
race 2	26#	13	14	9	10
race 3	9	18	13	22#	23#
race 4	9	4	0	17	24#

(*): data missing; +: "Pi" indicates the player's number. # indicates winner(s).

	Combination Race (Type II)				
	P1	P2	P3	P4	P5
race 9	17	6	7	20#	6
race 10	0	5	20#	–	7
race 11	6	6	5	28#	–

"Pi" indicates the player's number. # indicates winner.

	Combination Race (Type III)					
	P1	P2	P3	P4	P5	
race 5	23	21	20	21(1)	37(3)	(no winner)
race 6	18(1)	74(5)#	–	10	18	
race 7	23(1)#	37(1)	12	17(1)	17	
race 8	62(1)	16(2)	31	23	63(2)#	
race 12	21	30(2)#	20	21	19	

(declarations in brackets) # indicates winner.

and in three cases (race 6, race 10 and race 11), it was reduced to 4. Of the total number of 57 participants in the experiments, 3 decided not to enter the race, and 15 dropped out of the experiment before it ended (including the 5 participants in race 5 that had no winner).

The total cost varied greatly between different types of experiments, and in many cases (more than 50% of the total number of participants), players spent in excess of their participation fee[22]. In Table 3, we report the total number of trial combinations purchased in each type of experiment.

The data set we gathered shows many interesting features. We consider spending patterns first, for the winners and each type of loser (as defined in the previous section).

Spending Patterns Per Search Procedures

– the investment of the winner: in all cases the winner invested more than his/her participation fee, and in all cases but two (races 3 and 7), the winner invested more than the other players in the race.

The spending patterns however differed between types of experiments and were affected by the cost level. In all experiments of Type III and in experiments of Type I where players found and implemented a rule while playing, the winners increased their spending as their performance improved. In five races (1, 2, 9, 10, 11) with a deterministic information structure players invested in the first round in order to win directly in the second. It is interesting to notice that this behaviour closely resembles[23] pre-emptive behaviour by dominant firms. Particularly in experiments of Type II, the high search costs induced the winners to buy more trial combinations in the first round and also to reduce the number of trial combinations needed to discover the winning combination with certainty.

– the investment of losers (LP): this group of subjects have in general spending patterns similar to the winner, but their investment strategy is either less aggressive or their search is less lucky

– the investment of inexperienced players: inexperienced players invest an amount of resources that is dependent on how successful is their search during the race. They tend to invest more at the beginning and to decrease their spending when their performance does not improve. They drop out if they believe other subjects are going to win.

[22] The maximum amount spent by a participant (the winner in race 6) was £8.40, including the participation fee.

[23] From the questionnaire responses the subjects who participated in the second type of experiment, where the expected payoff of joint discovery was negative, preferred spending more in the first round, because the high cost of the search made it unprofitable to prolong the race.

– *the investment of the random players: random players invest at a low rate per round, varying their spending as their performance improves. These players drop out if the search is unsuccessful or if they believe someone else is going to win.*

– *Entry and Exit*

The questionnaire responses allowed an examination of the motivations of players who decided not to enter the competition. In all cases, the justification was the lack of a specific search strategy: in this circumstances, the current profit of £2.00 represented by the participation fee was preferred to the uncertain investment necessary to find the unknown combination.

Similarly, the decision to quit searching was dependent on the performance of the player during the search, especially when the participation fee had been spent[24]. Of all subjects who gave up, two were inexperienced players while the remaining were following apparently purely random strategies. The structure of information had no influence on the decision to enter the competition (the four subjects who did not join were all playing the deterministic version), but it did influence the exit decision, since the majority of players who dropped out were playing the noisy information version of the experiments.

– *Information*

From the questionnaire responses, we were able to analyse how subjects used the information regarding the other players' performance[25]. Only less than half of the total gave importance to the table reporting the number of correct letters guessed by each rival. The leader/winner was generally concerned only with their own speed, aiming to minimize the number of rounds. In two cases (Subject 4 in race 3 and Subject 5 in race 8), the winners had decided beforehand to stop the search if any other player had 6 correct letters in a combination.

In both cases, they realized while playing that such a score would have been irrelevant for winning, for some specific methods of solution or in the presence of random information. The majority of players attached importance to the table for two decisions: the decision to drop out and the decision on how many

[24] A large number of players did not hesitate to spend their own money, even if the search had been unsuccesful so far. Subject 1 in race 8 actually spent more than six pounds before quitting.

[25] Notice that the information structure of the experiments is deterministic and incomplete in the first and second case, and stochastic and incomplete in the third type of experiment.

combinations to buy in each round. Large investment in the early stages seemed to signal the potential winner, especially to those players who had entered the game with a not well developed strategy and invested little in the first stage, so that information could be processed more easily. In one case (Subject 4 in race 2), the player consulted the table to decide his own speed.

6 Nash Equilibrium

One question which inevitably springs to mind when analysing the results of this experiment is that of whether the actual behaviour of the participants is close to that specified by the relevant theory. Given that the experiment is a simultaneous-play interactive experiment the natural theoretical prediction is that specified by the Nash Equilibrium. So it is natural to inquire as to the nature and properties of the Nash Equilibrium in this particular game and whether it corresponds to some of the behaviour previously examined.

Unfortunately, this is far from easy, at least when there is more than one participant. (When there is just one, the solution is trivial, since the problem is no longer an interactive game: clearly the optimal thing for the participant to do – assuming an efficient combinatorial strategy is being used – is to buy just one trial combination per round. There are no economies of scale – so the purchase of more than one trial combination per round is simply inefficient.) When there are two or more participants, however, things get rather complicated – except in one rather special case. As has been demonstrated earlier in this paper, the purchase of 25 combinations (formed in one of the ways discussed above) is sufficient to discover the Winning Combination. It therefore follows that if the prize is sufficiently great relative to the cost of a trial combination to make simultaneous discovery of the Winning Combination by *all* participants at the beginning of the second round a profitable proposition, then a Nash equilibrium exists in which all participants buy 25 trial combinations in the first round. The condition is simple: that the prize divided by the number of participants is bigger than 25 trial costs. This is the situation of experiments of Type 1. So the Nash equilibrium prediction in those experiments is that all players buy 25 trial combinations in the first round and all simultaneously announce the Winning Combination at the start of the second round. Our results show that this Nash behaviour was displayed by 5 subjects out of 20 and only in two races out of 4 (the remaining races lasted 4 rounds and players bought a small number of combinations in the first round). So the Nash equilibrium prediction is *not* confirmed for the majority of participants in the Type 1 experiments.

In the Type 2 and Type 3 experiments, the simultaneous purchase of 25 combinations in the first round is no longer a Nash equilibrium. For in these experiments the cost of buying trial combinations was too large in relation to the prize to make this profitable: for if every one *did* buy 25 combinations in the first round, *they would all make negative profits*, since the prize divided by the number of participants is *less* than 25 trial costs. The next question is whether a different Nash equilibrium exists in these Types of experiment. Consider first Type 2 experiments and ignore for the moment the question of the most efficient combinatorial procedure. Concentrating solely on the issue of the optimum number of trial combinations in particular rounds *after the first*, we can see that this is a difficult task. The optimal number depends on a whole range of factors: the number of previous rounds, the information gained from the trial combinations in previous rounds, and the information matrix given to participants concerning the progress of the rival(s). Even if we concentrate solely on *symmetric* Nash Equilibria in pure strategies (there are quite clearly a number of – possibly uninteresting – *asymmetric* Nash Equilibria, for example, where all but one player drops out and the remaining player buys one trial combination per round) there are still rather formidable difficulties. Let $\mathbf{F}_{it}$ denote the above mentioned factors (those determining the optimal response) at the beginning of period t available to participant i; let n_{it} denote player i's response (in terms of the number of trial combinations purchased) in round t. Then the function $\phi_t(\cdot)$ provides a symmetric Nash Equilibrium response strategy if $n_{it} = \phi_t(\mathbf{F}_{it})$ is the best response by participant i given that all the other participants are responding with the purchase of n_{jt} combinations where $n_{jt} = \phi_t(\mathbf{F}_{jt})$ for all $j \neq i$. To compute such a symmetric Nash Equilibrium response function is a formidable task (because of the high dimensionality of the vector $\mathbf{F}$).

A slightly easier task is to enquire whether there exists a symmetric Nash Equilibrium response function (in pure strategies) of a rather simpler form. Let this be specified by a vector $\mathbf{n} = (n_1, n_2, n_3, n_4, n_5, n_6, \ldots)$ indicating the number of trial combinations to be purchased in rounds 1,2,3,4,5,6, ... (assuming the game has not yet terminated). Such a Nash Equilibrium response vector would exist if it could be shown that it was optimal for one participant to use this vector, given that all the other participants in the experiment were using the same vector. We have carried out a large number of simulations to discover whether this is indeed the case.

One obvious property of such a response vector would be that the (expected) profits for each participant would be zero. We can easily produce vectors which have this property. Unfortunately, it is equally easy to show that such a vector cannot be a Nash Equilibrium. For if one of the participants were to use $\mathbf{n} + (1, -1, 0, 0, 0, 0, \ldots)$ then that participant would earn positive expected profits while all the others would make negative expected profits. This immediately implies that there must be continuing pressure on all participants to buy more trial combinations in earlier rounds than the other participants. This process will continue until all subjects are buying enough combinations in the first round to *guarantee* discovery of the Winning Combination, in which case profits will become negative in the Type 2 experiments. In this Type of experiment, profits would be negative under this scenario, in which case this is not a Nash Equilibrium. (The situation is very remininscent of a Bertrand problem in which fixed costs in the Bertrand equilibrium yield negative overall profits.) So in the Type 2 race a symmetric Nash Equilibrium in pure strategies, even of this restricted form, does not exist.

Perhaps some examples would help illustrate this important point. Consider a prize of 25 and a trial cost of 30p. Suppose there are 5 players with each of them pre-committed to buying 4 combinations in each of rounds 1 through to 6 and 1 combination in round 7 (all, if necessary, of course). Simulations with 5000 repetitions show that player 1 earns −36p on average, player 2 8p, player 3 −5p, player 4 −18p, and player 5 5p. These average close to zero – which is a *necessary* but not *sufficient* condition for this strategy to be a symmetric Nash equilibrium. But now suppose that player 1 switches to a strategy of buying 5 combinations in the first round and 4 in each of 2 through to 6, whilst the other 4 players continue to use the strategy noted above. The simulation yields the following average profits: £2.21 to player 1, −49p to player 2, −51p to player 3, −76p to player 4 and −63p to player 5: a clear incentive to player 1 to switch to that strategy and a clear disincentive to players 2 to 5. Indeed all our simulations show that if one player buys more combinations in an earlier round than the other players, than that player makes a profit at the expense of the other players. Hence the non-existence of a symmetric Nash equilibrium in pure strategies for Type 2 experiment.

In such cases, one is naturally tempted into considering symmetric Nash Equilibrium in *mixed strategies*. In this case the response vector would be a *random* vector, possibly over the whole range of possible values for the response variable – though it is not clear that this is indeed the case. But if this *were* the case, it would be almost impossible to test empirically – at least without a *very* large number of experiments.

More importantly, however, the question of whether actual behaviour agrees with that specified by Nash Equilibrium behaviour misses the point. The essential point of *this* experiment, and essentially the reason why we set it up in this particular fashion, is that the decision problem is an extremely complex one. There are a number of dimensions of this complexity: first, the combinatorial strategy, second, the intensity of the strategy, and third the response strategy (to information gained by the participant herself and to information gained by the rivals). We believe that this complexity captures at least some of the essence of real-life R&D problems – in a manner that conventional economic theory (simple enough to allow a Nash Equilibrium strategy) does not.

Conclusion

Our experiments concern one aspect of technological change, that is the research competition for a patentable innovation, whose value is given and known. We have tried to examine this issue in a realistic framework in which skills, information and market competition affect the incentives to participate or to quit the race as well as the timing of investment.

There are a number of directions along which the research on these issues may be developed, namely the effect of the ease of imitation or licensing on the R&D rivalry, the incentive for R&D competitors to create joint ventures and the evolution of market structure in the presence of innovative opportunities and research competition. We believe that for each of these issues, experimental methods may provide significant insights and results on which new theoretical research may be based.

Appendix: Instructions for Experiments of Type I

The Combination Race (I)

Please read these instructions carefully and if you have any doubts ask the organiser before the experiment starts.

What is the Race About?

There are 5 participants in the Race. During the race, there will be, in a sealed envelope placed in full view of all participants, 7 slips of paper each containing a letter from the alphabet. These 7 letters will be randomly selected by the organiser at the beginning of the session and are known to the organiser and to no one else.

The Objective of the Race is to Discover the 7 Letters Written on the Slips of Papers

How Much Can you Win?

The participant who first discover the 7 letters will be paid the prize of 25 pounds. If more than one participant discovers the Winning Combination at the same time, those participants will equally share the prize. Once the Winning Combination is discovered, the Race is over. Non-winning participants do not receive any prize money, though they can take away with them what is left over from the participation fee of 2 pounds which is allocated to each participant at the start of the Race.

What are the Rules of the Combination Race?

The Race proceeds in a series of rounds. Each round lasts 8 minutes.

In each round you will type into a computer a set of zero, one or more combinations of 7 letters out of 26. The computer will tell you, for each trial combination typed, how many letters are in the Winning Combination, though you will not be told which of the letters actually appear. Of course, if all the 7 letters in any trial combination are in the Winning Combination, then that trial combination is the winning one – so you will then have discovered the Winning Combination.

Please remember that you are allowed up to two minutes to enter your trial combinations, one minute to change any of them and five minutes to look at your results and decide for the trial combinations you want to buy in the following round (time will be displayed on the screen). You also need to remember that the order of the letters is unimportant and repetitions are not allowed (there will be no repetition in the Winning Combination and the computer will not allow you to type combinations in which any of the letter is repeated).

An Example

If you want to buy two combinations, you will have to state that when the computer asks you to enter the number of trial combinations you wish to purchase: you will then type the two combinations you choose and on your screen will appear (for example):

ASDERTF 2
CFGTYUI 0

Which indicates that your first trial combination had two correct letters and the second one had none.

How Much will you have to Pay for your Trial Combinations?

For each trial combination you will have to pay a price of 10p. So, if you want to buy zero trial combination this will cost you nothing, if you buy one combination this will cost you 10p, and so on. The participation fee can be used to pay for this cost (notice that the fee allow you to buy a maximum of 20 combinations). You are however free to buy as many combination as you wish in excess of the participation fee. To this purpose, during the race, if you wish to buy trial combinations in excess of your participation fee, you will have to do so by paying the organiser the necessary amount. The computer will report the balance and display it before every purchase.

What Information will you be Given During the Race?

As already stated, you will be told how many letters are correct in your trial combinations at the end of each round.
Furthermore, the computer will also be able to tell you how many trial combinations have been purchased by each of the other participants and how many letters were reported correct in each of their trial combinations. The information is available on request at the beginning of each round, from the second one onwards. By pressing C when indicated, the computer will display a table like that below (this example considers just two players):

Total Number of Reported Correct Responses for Each Trial Combination

Subject number	Total comb.	0	1	2	3	4	5	6	7
1	10	5	3	0	2	0	0	0	0
2	3	3	0	0	0	0	0	0	0

this means that the first subject has bought 10 combinations in total, 5 of which had 0 correct letters, 3 had 1 correct letter and 2 had 3 correct letters. The second subject bought 3 combinations and none of them had any letter correct. Please notice that the time allowed to look at this table is not included in the time (8 minutes) allowed for each round.

How will the Race Proceed?

The mechanics of the Race are as follows. There will be a "practice race", before the Combination Race starts. The practice will allow you to get acquainted with the rules of the game. No prize will therefore be given and no cost will be charged for the trial combinations you want. Furthermore, to make things easier, in the "practice race", you will have to guess only 3 letters out of 26. Once the "practice race" is over, the Combination race will begin, and all participants will start the first round typing the trial combinations they wish to buy. After you type the trial combinations you can ask the computer to check how many letters are correct and wait for the next round to start. The Race will continue until the Winning Combination is discovered. The Winner(s) will then be paid in cash according to the above rules and the Race will be over.

You can withdraw from the Race at any time – taking with you what is left over from your participation fee.

References

Dasgupta P, Stiglitz J (1980b) Uncertainty, industrial structure and the speed of R&D. Bell Journal 11:1–28

Freeman C (1981) Economics of industrial innovation. Basingstoke, Penguin, London

Fudenberg D, Gilbert RJ, Stiglitz J, Tirole J (1983) Preemption, leapfrogging and competition in patent races, European Economic Review 22:3–31

Gilbert RJ, Newbery DMG (1982) Preemptive patenting and the persistence of monopoly. American Economic Review 72:514–526

Grossman GM, Shapiro C (1987) Dynamic R&D competition. Economic Journal 97:372–387

Harris C, Vickers J (1985) Perfect equilibrium in a model of a race. Review of Economic Studies 52:193–209

Hey JD, Reynolds ML (1991) Experiments, games and economics. In: Moss S and Rae J, *Artificial Intelligence and Economic Analysis*, Edward Elgar, Aldershot

Isaac MR, Reynolds SS (1988) Appropriability and market structure in a stochastic invention model. Quarterly Journal of Economics 103:647–671

Isaac MR, Reynolds SS (1992) Schumpeterian competition in experimental markets. Journal of Economic Behaviour and Organization 17:59–100.

Lee T, Wilde LL (1980) Market structure and innovation: A reformulation. Quarterly Journal of Economics 94:429–436

Levin R, Klevorich A, Nelson R, Winter S (1984) Survey research on R and D appropriability and technological opportunity, Part 1: Appropriability. Mimeo, Yale University

Loury GC (1979) Market structure and innovation. Quarterly Journal of Economics 93:395–410

Mansfield E, Schwartz M, Wagner S (1981) Imitation costs and patents: An empirical study. Economic Journal 91:907–918

Nelson R, Winter S (1982) An evolutionary theory of economic change. Harvard University Press Cambridge Mass

Nelson R (1987) Understanding technical change as an evolutionary process. North Holland
Reinganum JF (1989) The timing of innovation: Research, development and Diffusion. Handbook of Industrial Organization, Schmalansee R, Wllig RD (eds) Volume I. Elsevier Science Pub
Scherer FM (1980) Industrial market structure and economic performance. Chicago Rand McNally

Kolibri 360 GmbH
Ferdinand-Jühlke-Straße 7
99095 Erfurt, Deutschland
produktsicherheit@kolibri360.de